FOR FÜHRER AND FATHERLAND

SS MURDER AND MAYHEM IN WARTIME BRITAIN

RODERICK de NORMANN

A Sutton Publishing Book

This edition published in 1998 by Wrens Park Publishing, an imprint of
W.J. Williams & Son Ltd

First published in 1996 by Sutton Publishing Limited
Phoenix Mill · Thrupp · Stroud · Gloucestershire · GL5 2BU

British Library Cataloguing in Publication Data
A catalogue record for this book is available from the British Library

ISBN 0905 778 197

Typeset in 10/12pt Plantin
Typesetting and origination by
Sutton Publishing Limited
Printed in Great Britain by
WBC Limited, Bridgend, Mid-Glamorgan

CONTENTS

Dedicated to all those who died
so close to the light
at the end of their personal tunnels.

Acknowledgements

Where does one begin in a work of this sort, when those who have helped, advised, worked, even cajoled, are legion? If I have missed anyone out I do apologise.

To start, I must thank those who are still part of this story today; in particular Dick Hurn, who suffered my questioning on several occasions, and who has written the Foreword to this work. Also the former German prisoners of war still living in the United Kingdom: Mr Riedel, Erich Schoenfeld, Karl-Heinz Henning, Emil Flemming, Walter Herkstroeter and Paul Tauber; also Norbert Gladigau, Adam Mayer, Herman Heiner, Helmut Epstein and K.H. Przybylski who took the trouble to write to me from Germany.

I must also thank Pawel Bechler, a former member of 5 Polish Guard Company, and Mrs Bechler, a former Red Cross worker. Both still live close by the camp he once guarded and she once worked in. Arthur 'Mac' McKechnie from Chumleigh in Devon, a former Band Boy with the Second Battalion, Royal Wiltshire Regiment, has also been inspirational and full of encouragement.

Further afield, my grateful thanks must go to Peter Everett, presently working in Bristol for the BBC. His research and production of the documentary 'The Black and the Grey' in 1984 produced a mass of information which he allowed me to use. In particular, his archival notes regarding Colonel Wilson in Comrie Camp and the translations of some of the Sulzbach Papers were invaluable.

In Devizes, now my own home town, I was always kept on the right track by those who themselves had lived through the war. In particular I would like to thank Albert 'Charlie' May, a virtual goldmine of information, as well as Len Reeves, who suggested a number of good contacts. Joy Pride, Jim Gaiger's niece, also has my thanks for her detailed accounts of those days.

I should also mention Lorna Haycock of the Devizes Local History Society and the Devizes Museum, as well as Jim Girvan, Bill Underwood and David Knapman. As regards the Devizes railway, which played a key role in the story, I must thank Rod Priddle and wish him luck with his own book, as well as Lil Painter and Eric Slade who used to work there during the war. Also a special thank-you to Doug Richards, a former Welsh Guardsman at the London Cage.

In Scotland, I owe a big debt of gratitude to the McCullochs, father and son, as well as to James McLeod, presently serving in Bosnia as a TA Signaller. Also Alexander Budge who, alongside Class 7 at Hillhead School in Wick, produced the most excellent *In Enemy Hands* and allowed me to use extracts from their interviews. At the same time, I must also thank Stuart Smith who undertook some of the ground work in Comrie itself and Mr W.F. Will who lent me his copy of the BBC programme 'The Black and The Grey'.

To the staffs working so hard in some of the nation's archives and collections, my gratitude is also due. As always, such a book could not be written without recourse to the Public Record Office at Kew. Material quoted from their files is Crown copyright and, as always, is reproduced with the permission of the Controller of Her Majesty's Stationery Office. I could not have made use of the documents without the help and direction of Mr I.D. Goode, the Deputy Departmental Record Officer at the Ministry of Defence who went so far as to review, and open, closed files on my behalf.

Of course, it goes without saying that the resources at the Imperial War Museum in London were excellent, especially the Sound Archives Department whose recordings are unique. The same must be said of the Trustees of the Liddell Hart Centre for Military Archives in London who gave permission for me to use the Sulzbach letters in their collection.

Closer to home, a very big thank-you must also go to the Wiltshire Record Office at Trowbridge. Without their permission to use material from the Wiltshire Constabulary files, this story would have been sadly incomplete. The same can be said of the Liverpool Constabulary who helped me with information concerning Colonel Wilson, the former Commander at Comrie Camp. Thanks must also go to Major Geoffrey Crook of the Royal Pioneer Corps Association and to Major John Stirling who allowed me access to his extensive files on the one thousand-plus Pioneer companies that existed during the war!

As regards the RAF Yatesbury material, thanks must go to Mr Eddie Brown and son, who recently formed the Yatesbury Association, and to Colin Latham, Ron Arnold and Ted Vogel, all former members of No. 9 Radio School. At the same time, a special thanks to Alfred Daltrey, Mrs Frank Ockenden and Mrs A. Toogood.

All the accounts from 8 Para with regards to the arrest of the Devizes ringleaders are due to Dr Tony Leake who put me in contact with a multitude of former B Company members, including Jim Wheeler, Frank Ockenden, G. Bird, T. Hopkins, Harry Gosling (who now lives in Australia) and Peter Roberts. My thanks must also go to Colonel Alistair Wilson, Ted George and A.A. Byland, all former members of 6 Airborne Armoured Reconnaissance Regiment.

Abroad, a very big thank-you to Bob Cox of the American Legion Headquarters who put me in touch with former members of both the US 4th Armored Division, especially Harry Feinberg, as well as 128 General Hospital. Also to the American National Archives in Washington DC who allowed me to use several War Diaries from units stationed close by. In Germany, I must also thank the German Old Comrades Association who, through their magazine *Alte Kameraden* enabled me to contact several former prisoners. The same thanks must also go to the Old Comrades Associations of the Waffen-SS and Fallschirmjaeger for publishing requests for information.

Finally, a very big thank-you to my father-in-law, Alon Pritchard, for his German translations and to my parents for their proofreading of the initial manuscript.

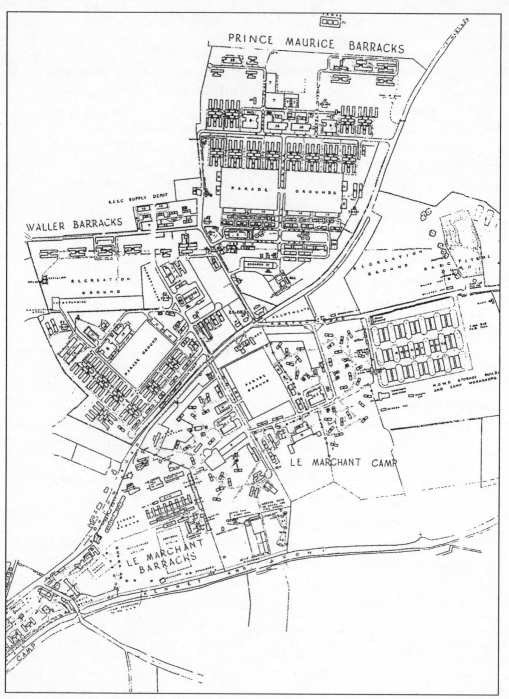

The Devizes Camp Area, 1943.

Introduction

To suffer the indignity of being a prisoner of war – for indignity it really is for most – must be soul-destroying. For the German Waffen-SS, so long brought up to believe in the invincibility of the Führer, the Party and the Fatherland, it was often devastating. Consequently, in many POW camps both in Britain and abroad, they continued their fight, often against their own countrymen.

The story you are about to read is a true one. I have done my utmost to ensure accuracy despite the fact that, at the time, events were deeply shrouded in rumour and hearsay owing to strict censorship. These rumours have persisted up to the present day.

As far as I can ascertain, the first public account of the story appeared in Colonel Alexander Scotland's book, *The London Cage*, published in 1957. Colonel Scotland was at the centre of the investigation into the so-called 'Devizes Plot' and the subsequent hunt for Wolfgang Rosterg's killers. Unfortunately, his published account does not match the reports he and his staff wrote at the time. I have not been able to discover the reason for this. Other historians and writers, with little else to go on, have embellished the story, some reaching ridiculous levels of German intrigue and plot that have very little recorded evidence to support them.

None the less, the true story is both fascinating and frightening. It is a story that records, for some at least, a fight between Good and the Evil that was embodied in National Socialism. Good won. It won through the professional dedication of individuals who stood for the good of the Allied cause, paving the way for the so-called re-education programmes that ultimately allowed the post-war Germany to become what it is today. God forbid that any generation ever has to experience such trauma again.

Roderick de Normann
Devizes, April 1996

CHAPTER ONE

Take an Englishman and a German

Learn all you can about the German Army,
and one day you will be a valuable man
to your country.[1]

On 3 September 1939, when the British Prime Minister Neville Chamberlain was faced with no option but to declare war on Germany, Alexander Paterson Scotland was approaching his sixtieth birthday. As far back as 1903, Scotland had been closely involved in all things German. In South-West Africa – today Namibia – he was caught up in the Hottentot rebellion while working for the trading company South African Territories Limited, also known as S.A.T. Ltd. Based in the small town of Ramonsdrift, on the border of the Cape Colony and German South-West Africa, Scotland had first arrived in South Africa with the intention of joining his brother and fighting the Boers. By the time he got there, however, the war was over: '. . . there was nothing for it but to resume, in a new land, the unexciting pursuits of a civilian clerk . . .', he was to write later in his autobiography, *The London Cage*.[2]

Although the British war with the Boers – the second Boer War – was concluded in 1902, there was still much disquiet in the region. Local tribes had seen how the Cape Dutch had successfully taken on the British and they too rose up against their colonial masters. The Hottentots in particular were to conduct a tough four-year campaign against the Germans – and it was into this colonial war that Scotland found himself drawn.

Towards the end of 1903, S.A.T. Ltd moved its trading post from Ramonsdrift to Warmbad. The German forces soon became the principal customers and in particular were buying biscuits, soft drinks and canned foods. Although business was good, Scotland soon found that his inability to speak either German or Cape Dutch put him at a disadvantage. He was strongly advised to learn German by the local commandant, one Hans von Quitzow. Scotland did so and was soon called for again:

> One day, von Quitzow came to me with a proposition. The bulky cases of provisions we supplied to his troops . . . had to be distributed to the soldiers by a specially appointed officer at a time when German manpower was sorely strained. Von Quitzow's proposal was that I should become that officer, signing up with the garrison force as a German soldier.[3]

Indeed, so keen was the German commandant to have Scotland on his payroll that he had already drawn up the necessary documentation. All it required was Scotland's signature. He signed.

Scotland served with the German Army for nearly four years, even being issued with a uniform and rifle. A *Kriegsfreiwilliger*, or 'war-volunteer', he was responsible for getting the supplies up to the German soldiers fighting in the bush and was so proficient that at the end of the campaign he was awarded the Order of the Red Eagle for his services. At the same time, Scotland's work did not go unnoticed by the British authorities back in Cape Town. Summoned to a meeting at Government House with Dr L.S. Jameson, the Prime Minister of the Cape Colony, Scotland was thoroughly questioned as to his activities. Scotland was to write much later:

> He listened closely to my detailed replies, and then said: 'I've decided to make you the General Manager, unpaid, of the Cape Government trading post at Ramonsdrift. You will be the authority for deciding on permits for the goods allowed to cross the Orange River. As an officer of my department, you will be responsible only to me.'[4]

Thus, for the first time, Alexander Scotland found himself working for the British Intelligence Community in South Africa, reporting direct to Cape Town and to agents working for General Smuts, who by 1910 was the Minister of Defence in General Botha's first Union Cabinet. Now able to speak fluent, military German, he could travel freely. This enabled him not only to send back to Cape Town details of the German dispositions throughout their colony, but also to start to understand the German military mentality. This was especially useful as Britain and Germany started to slide towards war in 1914.

War, when it came, brought a sharp shock to Scotland. Because he was English, all the German trust that he had built up, collapsed. Just days after the declaration of war he was arrested by the German colonial police in Warmbad. After they had searched his house in Keetmanshoop, he was imprisoned in Windhoek, where he remained until July 1915. Repeatedly interrogated, Scotland was to say of this interlude:

> During the long, arduous questioning I was given by the staff officer attached to the German colonial troops, I learned perhaps the most valuable lesson of all my career in South Africa. From that officer, a Lieutenant Hepka, I acquired some of the techniques of interrogating an enemy subject.[5]

Eventually released, Scotland made his way back to England, determined to continue his intelligence work where it would be most useful. On arrival in London, he approached the War Office but was flatly turned down. He next tried the Admiralty, but again to no avail. Finally, he found himself before a selection board of the Inns of Court Regiment at Lincoln's Inn Fields. Sitting before two generals, Scotland was brusquely informed that the regiment was full. If he was to be allowed to join, he would have to have a recommendation from a very senior man. To that end, could he name one? Without much hesitation, Scotland asked if General Smuts in South Africa would be senior enough. Several days later, General Smuts did indeed furnish a recommendation and Scotland was enlisted as a private.

General Smuts' recommendation again brought Scotland's name to the attention of the War Office. Within weeks of starting his basic training, he was called forward to attend a course in Intelligence at Horse Guards in London. He sailed through the language proficiency tests and then faced yet another board of senior officers. When asked what he knew about the German Army, Scotland was able to tell them that he had actually served in it! Within weeks, he found himself called forward for 'Special Duties in France' with the rank of Second Lieutenant.

Scotland was ordered to report to General Headquarters in France where his first task was to question some three thousand prisoners being held outside Le Havre. Army Intelligence was worried that the Germans had developed a system of rehabilitation that allowed them to return their wounded to the front line more quickly than the British or French. If this were so, did it indicate a shortage of manpower?

Scotland stated later that '. . . it was a strange moment, facing the three thousand Germans . . . I realised also that I was falling quite naturally into the manner of a German officer . . .'.[6] Scotland first ordered the prisoners to divide themselves up by unit. Next, he ordered the senior NCOs to take down all the details from those men who had been wounded and had passed through hospital prior to their capture. Within two hours Scotland had the information he required to answer GHQ's question. By midnight the same day, he had dispatched his first report to GHQ by messenger.

Three weeks went by and he heard nothing. Then, out of the blue, he was summoned to the Senior Mess for lunch.

> Wondering whether I was due for a severe dressing-down, I went along to the Senior Mess to find myself seated at lunch in the company of the Brigadier, some twelve to fifteen generals and major-generals, and not a man below the rank of Colonel. I was still a Second Lieutenant . . .[7]

After lunch a somewhat tense Scotland was questioned as to how he had found out what he did and in such a short time? The senior officers just could not believe that the information was correct. Scotland explained what he had done and why. But the generals wondered, since the information had been collected by German NCOs, whether it could be reliable. Scotland assured them that he had checked the results himself before putting pen to paper and found it to be correct. He himself had done very little, apart from collating the raw information. GHQ was genuinely impressed with his efforts and Scotland found himself readily accepted into GHQ. He was even given the rather grandiose title 'Expert for Manpower Information on the German Army'.

Scotland was to remain in GHQ for the remainder of the war, both interrogating prisoners and instigating attempts to cross the German lines to seek out information. But it was in the field of interrogation that Scotland really made his name. He wrote:

> From my Headquarters in the École Militaire at Montreuil-sur-Mer I would . . . be producing on paper, with graphs, sketches and detailed lists, the picture that revealed how the German units were made up – what were the different military categories, what were their jobs in the line, what was disclosed by the captured letters telling of home conditions, and so on. As head of our manpower control unit I was completely mobile, moving freely along the front whenever conditions suggested that promising information might be forthcoming.[8]

Scotland was very much master of his own domain, evolving interrogation techniques that were to become the standard some twenty-five years later, during the Second World War. One case involved the interrogation of a German Oberleutnant who had arrived at a prisoner of war (POW) camp with a letter from the Australian unit that had captured him. This letter stated that Oberleutnant Kastel had shown supreme courage commanding a machine-gun section that had held the Australians up for nearly four days. In recognition of this brave feat of arms, his captors wanted him to be treated well.

Intrigued, Scotland decided to talk to the man himself. He was faced with a problem, however. He could not simply enter the prisoners' compound and call him across as his fellow prisoners might have suspected him of collaboration. This in turn would hardly have put the prisoner at ease. Instead, Scotland announced, in his by now perfect German, that he wanted to discuss the gallantry shown by the prisoner and recorded by his Australian captors. By pure luck, Scotland discovered that the Oberleutnant had been born and brought up in German South-West Africa, in the small town of Gibeon. Knowing it well, Scotland was soon deep in conversation with the prisoner. Totally at his ease, Kastel was unaware that Scotland had several members of his staff hidden around the room with notebooks and pens, there being no reliable microphones in those days.

★ ★ ★

On 8 August 1914, while Alexander Scotland had been languishing in his Windhoek prison cell, a young German Jew by the name of Herbert Sulzbach joined the queues outside his local recruiting office in Frankfurt-am-Main in western Germany. Born in 1894 into a rich German banking family, Sulzbach later described his father as 'a modest millionaire'.[9] Sulzbach found himself in the 63rd Frankfurt Field Artillery Regiment and by September 1914 was manning a gun in France. He remained with his regiment until the Armistice in November 1918.

Sulzbach survived all those bloody Western Front battles. In 1914 his guns supported the initial German successes at Lille, before moving on towards Armentières and digging in for what was to become trench warfare. Some sixty years later he wrote:

> I – and I believe all of us who are still alive – can remember every day of those months on the Western Front as if it happened yesterday. Strange again, that we do not 'look back in anger' but in a kind of nostalgia when we speak of Armentières, Ypres, Champagne, Picardie, Somme, Chemin-des-Dames, St Quentin and all these places we knew so well where, when having a rest in little villages behind the front line, we made real friends with the French population. They were nice to us, not only because we gave them food, but because they saw in us the soldiers who did their duty. I always claim that this 'our' war was the last knightly war ever fought, knightly because we respected the enemy and he respected us.[10]

Commissioned in late 1917, Sulzbach and his regiment were part of the divisional artillery train to the 19th Jaeger Infantry Division when the German 'March Offensive' was unleashed against the British, Colonial and French troops in 1918. Initially successful, the offensive eventually ground to a halt, just as Hitler's Ardennes Offensive would do some twenty-six years later. By July, the Germans, now also facing American troops, were on the defensive, despite the large numbers of reinforcements made available through the collapse of the Russian front after the Bolshevik Revolution. Of the final Armistice, Sulzbach was to say:

> It was in France on the retreat from the last terrific battle near Etreux when I, as a young Lieutenant and Adjutant of a German light artillery battalion, had to read this depressing order to my men. The war was over.

But we, the German front-line soldiers of 1914 . . . could hardly believe in defeat, although the disaster for us started on July 16 1918, when out of the Bois de Villers-Cotterets, the Allied forces, the Americans for the first time in masses, attacked our lines after the failure of our last and third offensive near Reims.

For the first time we saw the baby tanks smashing through our infantry lines, and our retreat during the night over the River Vesle was difficult indeed, but I managed to get my three batteries into our next position without any losses.[11]

What Sulzbach did not mention was that he was awarded the Iron Cross First Class for his efforts that day. Indeed, his gun batteries had been firing over open sights at the light tanks and had only just managed to withdraw. Sulzbach himself had been in the thick of it.

For the majority of Germans, including Sulzbach, the Armistice was a grave disappointment. In a taped interview at the Imperial War Museum in London he stated:

I was depressed, as most Germans, about these humiliating conditions of unconditional surrender . . . Germany didn't deserve Versailles . . . [and] these were partly the basis on which Hitler started . . .[12]

Sulzbach was luckier than most when he went home. Despite Germany's defeat, his father's bank was still viable and making money. In order to settle his son, Sulzbach's father bought a paper mill near Berlin and put him in charge of it. Herbert Sulzbach dutifully took up the challenge, and moved out from the family home in Frankfurt in 1920. How successful a manager he was is not recorded, but he and his firm survived the Depression and the rampant inflation of the Weimar Republic. Then, in 1933, Adolf Hitler and the National Socialist Party came to power.

For Sulzbach, the trouble started almost straight away. In 1932 he had written a letter to his local newspaper complaining about, and in the final paragraph denouncing, Hitler and all he and his party stood for. After the successful elections, Sulzbach was informed that his letter had not gone unnoticed. Slowly the pressures began to build, first against his business and then against himself and Mrs Sulzbach, the niece of the famous conductor Otto Klemperer. The writing was very much on the wall for the Sulzbachs and when his Berlin paper company was compulsorily bought by the government for a pittance in 1936, they made the decision to leave. In 1937 Herbert Sulzbach legally emigrated to Britain, finding a very comfortable flat in London at Belgrave Park Gardens. Indeed the flat was big enough for two of the bedrooms to be rented out to lodgers. In 1938 Sulzbach returned to Germany to collect his wife and her sister, along with their remaining furniture. This is not so surprising, for the relatively well-off Sulzbach had paid all the expenses during his own emigration process. When he left, however, his remaining assets were frozen.[13] This led to some difficulties the following year, as Matthew Sullivan described in his book *Thresholds of Peace*:

> The removal men showed him where in his furniture he could safely hide some currency, but he did not dare to risk it. His faith in a humane Germany was . . . confirmed when they said farewell to the braver members of their friendship circle. A local policeman, for all the swastika in his badge of office, forged his wife's passport and then risked his job by coming to the little party they gave in a pub. This man, Wachmeister Oetzel, whose name Herbert Sulzbach was to celebrate again and again in later life, became for him the symbol of the permanent and true Germany.[14]

During the year between their arrival in Britain and the start of the Second World War on 1 September 1939, Herbert Sulzbach and his wife led a quiet life. One initial attraction was that his Berlin company had a subsidiary in Slough; Sulzbach tried to keep it going but to no avail and it was finally wound up in 1940.

Prior to coming to London, he had written an account of his First World War experiences and he now set about trying to have them published in England. In his search for a publisher, he came across the writing of one Captain Basil Liddell Hart. This well known historian and military thinker was by now best known for his writings about the usage of tanks and tank warfare. Sulzbach first wrote to Liddell Hart after reading one of his books on the Western Front. In a later letter to Liddell Hart in 1942, Sulzbach wrote:

> I know nearly all the places and battlefields you describe in the book you sent me, as I fought in France for 4 years and 2 months, and all these places are mentioned in my own book. The year 1918 makes half of my

book. As I fought from 21-3-18, taking off in St Quentin against the 5th English Army, I sent my book to Sir Philip Gibbs and his criticism was most flattering.

When I offered my book in this country, having come here as a refugee in May 1937, it was too late for a book of the last war. Do you really think that an opportunity might still come? It would be very helpful for me, but its contents are so contrary to my hatred of to-day![15]

With war fast approaching during the summer of 1939, Herbert Sulzbach volunteered to join the British Army but was turned down flat – he was, after all, a German. Again in 1940 he tried to join up, but this time through the various Governments in Exile that were to be found in London after their countries had been invaded. Another extract from the same letter to Liddell Hart illustrates the frustration Sulzbach must have felt at the time:

I offered my services on August 27th 1939 to the Government and volunteered for the R.A. (having had command of a battery in 1916). Then I volunteered in 1940, offering my services to France, Belgium, Holland and Norway when they were invaded – but no country said 'Yes'.[16]

Towards the end of the so-called 'Phoney War', Sulzbach was still trying to launch his literary career with his memoirs, as well as writing to various daily newspapers with his views of the situation as it unfolded. On 21 May 1940, for instance, he wrote to the editor of the *Daily Telegraph* with his views on Marshal Petain, the French hero of Verdun in 1918 and the French traitor in 1940. But writing letters and expressing his views was to work against Sulzbach after the fall of France in June 1940.

With Paris captured and the division of France in full swing, the greatest fear in London was that of invasion. Rumours and stories of German blitzkrieg tactics abounded. The use of German paratroop soldiers against the Netherlands and the fall of the 'unconquerable' Fort Eban-Emael on the Maginot Line all added fuel to the fire. Perhaps most disturbing of all were the accounts of German troops dressed as refugees, or even nuns, in order to infiltrate behind the Allied lines. Britain readied herself for possible invasion.

One measure that could be taken, however, was to round up all potential spies and aliens. Internment tribunals were hastily set up. The Sulzbachs and the majority of the other refugees who had fled Germany in the late 1930s were ordered to report to their local police stations for questioning under Internment Rule 18B. Herbert Sulzbach and his wife went before a magistrate at Bow Street, but they failed to convince the authorities of their refugee status primarily, according to Sulzbach, because the police found a copy of a letter he had written in 1923 to his aunt, complaining of the French annexation of the Rhurgebeit under the Versailles Treaty agreements. In the letter was the phrase '. . . the Allies will regret it . . .'. This was enough.

On 31 May 1940 Herbert Sulzbach – having spent three nights in a cell at Bow Street – and his wife, were given just half an hour to pack some bags before heading into internment. Herbert was sent into internment at Onchan on the Isle of Man but Mrs Sulzbach was not so fortunate: she had to endure four weeks in Holloway prison before she too, went into internment on the Isle of Man, but in a different camp from her husband, at Port Erin. For several months they did not even know of each other's whereabouts. At the same time, to add the final insult to the injury, their flat in London was bombed and burnt out. They lost everything save the few things they took into internment.[17]

Although internment must have been a bitter pill for Herbert Sulzbach to swallow, his stoical nature came to the fore. Sailing from Liverpool after spending a night in a local Army barracks, Sulzbach found himself confined in a requisitioned boarding house with twenty other internees. 'I suppose most of them were Jewish', he was to later recount. Of the twenty, there appeared to be only one real Nazi, an Austrian room-waiter who had been working at the Savoy Hotel in London: 'he was a 100% Nazi', Sulzbach recalled. Others had seen it all before: 'I was also with a chap who was interned in the same place in the First War . . . a Mr Hertzog'.

The daily routine was not so bad, save for the food 'which was horrible, just a herring a day'. Guarded by soldiers from the Pioneer Corps, the internees soon began to organise their camp routines. Among them were many scholars, doctors and journalists. 'One of the journalists was a man called Hess who worked for

Ullstein . . . he became a soldier under the name of Hudson.' Soon, throughout the camp, thriving committees and classes were to be found, as some of the more eminent internees turned to teaching others who wanted to learn, if only to pass the time. Sulzbach found himself on the 'University Committee' while others joined the Concert Committee under the world-renowned pianist Dr Freidman.

In all the Internment Camps in the British Isles, there was a screening campaign to root out all the undesirable 'aliens' being held. The campaign entailed a series of interviews designed to gauge whether or not the internee held true Nazi sympathies. Those who 'failed' faced the prospect of being shipped to Australia or Canada. In due course, Herbert Sulzbach was called forward:

> One day I was interviewed by Lieutenant Napier, who was the camp Intelligence Officer. He asked me lots of things. Also about . . . Hitler and he realised I was not a Nazi. Thanks to this interview I was not sent to Canada or Australia . . .[18]

As with many of those interned, Sulzbach longed to become fully involved in fighting the very party that had made him a refugee from his own country. Those who passed the screening test were eligible to join up into the Pioneer Corps. Over ten thousand men did just that, many later transferring into other arms and services. Using aliases to disguise their identities should they fall into German hands, many of these internees went on to show true gallantry in action or behind enemy lines. In the autumn of 1940 Herbert Sulzbach put his name forward, if only to escape the onset of boredom at Onchan. Presenting himself to the Recruiting Officer who now appeared in the camp regularly, Sulzbach was accepted into the Pioneer Corps. On 10 October 1940 he walked through the Onchan camp gates for the last time with a military railway warrant to Bradford in his pocket. Sulzbach's hopes were very high, primarily because he could now be united with his wife again, after the five-month separation. But it was not to be:

> We had been promised that as soon as one of us joined up, they promised that the other would be released at once. It took three months . . .[19]

Once in Bradford, Private Sulzbach underwent basic rudimentary training and then, because there was still a very real threat of invasion, he was set to work digging trenches and building tank-traps all along the south coast with 229 Pioneer Company, whose headquarters was in Didcot. This company held many such former refugees as himself who were often caught up in the bombing of such towns as Plymouth and Portsmouth. He also found himself working in Devizes, a market town just north-east of Salisbury Plain and its Army training grounds. Here, for the first time since leaving Germany, he saw German soldiers – prisoners – working in the fields. 'I did not see them as people at all, I only saw the swastika on their uniforms', he said.[20] Little did Sulzbach know how significant Devizes was to be for him towards the end of the war.

★ ★ ★

During the inter-war years, Alexander Scotland had not been idle. Returning to South-West Africa after the Armistice in November 1918, he took up once again his managerial post with South Africa Territories Ltd. He remained in southern Africa until 1927 when he and his wife Roma were posted to South America. For six years, he toured the vast continent, visiting many of the emerging countries such as Argentina, Brazil and Uruguay. Still very much involved with monitoring the local German populations, once his enemies, he later wrote about this period:

> Everywhere I made discreet enquiries about the considerable German communities in South America, and about their widespread activities. The place was the proverbial hotbed of intrigue and espionage, complete with exotic women, ruthless undercover men, fabulous parties of diplomats and businessmen and secret agents working in the embassies, consulates and head offices of cities large and small.
>
> These were truly the cloak, and sometimes dagger, days of the pre-war years. As far as the German communities were concerned, I soon learned that it was almost a matter of routine for a German national to be in touch with some Government or consular official who would be able to 'use' his services . . . for whatever German-inspired purposes might be decreed.[21]

In 1933, after he and his wife had returned to Britain, Scotland made a long tour throughout Germany. While in Stuttgart, they called on a German acquaintance by the name of Hauptman Schmidt. Scotland had got to know Schmidt in South America when the latter used to visit in his capacity as the representative from the 'Colonial Institute'. Scotland soon realised that this was not all Schmidt was involved with:

> What intrigued me more than anything else, however, was the discovery that the [Hauptman's] busy little 'Colonial Institute' was in fact an important centre of control for the activities of Germans living overseas. Later, it became the active information centre for directing the work of agents and fifth columnists in many parts of the world, notably in Africa and South America.

By 1937 Scotland was convinced that Hitler and the Nazis would once more bring war to Europe. He wrote after that war:

> From a large variety of German friends, Jewish and otherwise, I was learning by 1935 how the shape of the Gestapo and the SS was being evolved. And so, by 1937, again visiting Germany, I watched the spectacle of a country gone mad.[22]

The trip in 1937 was to reveal to Scotland more than just 'a country gone mad' for, quite unexpectedly, he was summoned to meet the Führer himself.

While in Munich, Scotland visited an old friend from his South-West Africa days. Declining to name him in his autobiography except as 'Herr K., who is dead now', Scotland described how he was pumped for information regarding his dealings with the German colonial administrators during the Hottentot uprising. The next day, Scotland was again called in his hotel by 'Herr K.' who wanted to know more. So persistent was the gentleman that he sent a car to collect Scotland. On arrival, Scotland was ushered into a drawing-room to meet some of 'Herr K.'s colleagues. Scotland described what happened next:

> As coffee was brought in and about to be poured, the door opened. In walked Hitler with two bespectacled associates whose names were not mentioned when I was introduced.

The Führer was strangely direct and purposeful in his attitude. Unsmiling, he looked at and through me, almost searching, it seemed, for some specific item of information about my character. . . .

His opening words were certainly unexpected: 'Sit here, please,' he ordered, indicating one of the chairs. I felt some amusement at this immediate command over the furniture in another man's house.[23]

Hitler questioned Scotland, so it seems, for some considerable time. He wanted clarification on his work in Africa and America, to know whether he was still a serving army officer, even how old he was. Just as quickly as the meeting had started, so it finished. Hitler just rose and left. At the door, however, he stopped and turned. 'You are an ingenious man, Schottland. Now I can understand the reports we have on our files about you,' he said.[24]

By the beginning of 1940, Scotland was accepting 'more or less gracefully the idea that I was militarily unemployable'. Then, one early March morning, Scotland received a message that was to change his life for the next ten years or so:

One day a telephone call from the War Office demanded my prompt attendance for an interview. There I learned that General Mason-Macfarlane, chief of our Intelligence in the field, had flashed a message from France asking that I be called in without delay to give advice on the subject of interrogation.

So, on a windy March morning, I flew to France. Carrying major's crowns on my 25-year-old tunic . . . I landed at Arras, reported to GHQ, and straight away got to work.[25]

The newly promoted Major Scotland was tasked with establishing the prisoner of war control and interrogation structures that would be required if Germany attempted to invade the Low Countries and France. Based at Dieppe with a staff of one, he also had to perform the duties of the local security officer. After the German attack in May of that year, Scotland soon found himself concentrating on the security aspects of the mass of refugees fleeing before the German tanks instead of interrogating captured German soldiers. By the time he was evacuated, Major Scotland had just eighteen prisoners in his care.

CHAPTER TWO

The Shock of Capture

When by the labour of my 'ands
I've helped to pack a transport tight
With prisoners for foreign lands
I ain't transported with delight.

Rudyard Kipling[1]

Capture in battle is, on the whole, a traumatic experience. Often prisoners have had to endure bloody combat before they are forced to lay down their arms. Around them there may be the sights, smells and sounds of their comrades horribly mutilated or badly wounded, crying out in pain. They themselves may be totally unhurt, leading to a rapid guilt-complex: 'Why am I still alive when my friends are dead?' Such complexes lead very quickly to the feeling of having let down those around them, something soldiers feel very keenly. Another component of the trauma is the quiet that descends over a battlefield once the fighting is over. Usually, combat is incredibly loud, with detonations from artillery, guns, mortars and perhaps even bombs. The upsurge of adrenalin helps the mind to shut out the normal reaction to such cacophony. But once the battle is over, the absence of noise becomes deafening in itself. Ears ring and the smallest of sounds, even a bird singing, can be heard with the utmost clarity.

Another facet of the shock often results in captives needing desperately to share their experiences with others. They need comfort and support to come to terms with the fact that they have survived while others have not. Prisoners recently captured can often not stop talking. They will talk with anyone willing to show the slightest interest, sometimes even with themselves. In contrast, others lapse into total silence, in a condition very akin to being heavily drugged. This is usually caused by the realisation that it is all over: no longer will they have to endure the rigours and bloodshed that have gone before. It is finished.

All of these emotions lead to what is termed today the 'shock of capture' and it is this condition that interrogators use to their advantage to glean valuable intelligence. Prisoners have to be questioned as soon as possible. They need to be brought quickly out of danger and into a system where everything appears to be controlled very smoothly, where everyone in authority appears to know exactly what he or she is doing. There is no fear any more, just the awful realisation that they have fallen into the hands of their enemy and that they have no idea what will happen next.

Major Scotland knew all of this very well. He had experienced it himself in South-West Africa and he had employed it during the First World War. Now, at the age of sixty, he was being asked to reteach the lessons to the British Expeditionary Force in France, and later its remnants in England. Scotland had this to say about the state of Britain's preparedness to receive and use captured personnel:

> Surprising as it may seem, the fact was that, at the beginning of the Second World War, the British Army was woefully ill-equipped for the skilled tasks of interrogation, security and Intelligence in the field. The shortage in trained officers and men continued indeed right up to the end of hostilities, but the position at the start of the war was pathetically inadequate. With the exception of one or two men who had gained an apprenticeship in Intelligence from 1914 to 1918, no serving officer of 1939 had received any training.[2]

Scotland's words were a sorry indictment indeed, but not wholly accurate. The War Office had been looking at some of the problems that they envisaged might be encountered. As far back as 1918, the War Office had realised that for Intelligence to be used successfully, any Intelligence staff needed to work closely with its neighbouring operational staff. Unfortunately, after the Armistice in 1918 and the large-scale demobilisation that took place, such a concept was not easy to bring to fruition as the Intelligence staffs were some of the first to be cut. Indeed, the then fledgling Intelligence Corps was disbanded completely. Consequently, it was not until June 1937 that an Operational Intelligence Centre (OIC) was seriously considered. Although the Munich Crisis of 1938 added some impetus to the plan, it was not until February 1939 that the OIC became a reality. Unfortunately at the time, the War Office itself did not control the joint information collection, collation, analysis or distribution of Intelligence. Rather, as had occurred in the First World War, the War Office was responsible for long-term background information and the administration of the Military Intelligence Branches only. It was up to the Intelligence staffs in the field to produce operational and tactical intelligence for use by the commanders.

Here again there was a drawback. During the inter-war years, Intelligence posts in battalions and above were not considered the height of achievement. Often commanders, too, did not feel that the Intelligence posts within their staffs were as important, let's say, as those of Command appointments. Consequently, at the outbreak of war in 1939, many Intelligence posts were poorly staffed with trained personnel, if staffed at all. Indeed, when the British Expeditionary Force (BEF) deployed to France, its small GHQ Intelligence staff was a mix of all sorts, cobbled together with the help of MI5.

Sensing the growing and urgent need to set up some form of unified approach to the Intelligence problems, the Chiefs of Staff proposed a Situation Report Centre that would include representatives from all three defence ministries, the Directorate of Intelligence and the Foreign Office. Working alongside another body, the Joint Intelligence Committee (JIC), it ensured Intelligence requirements could be met at an operational level.[3]

Apart from basic field intelligence, a range of other means was investigated as a supplement to general Intelligence work. The foremost of these was the Government Code and Cipher School (GC&CS), breaking enemy signal codes, the Intelligence from which became known as ULTRA. Much has since become known about ULTRA and Bletchley Park, the heart of the operation. Suffice it to say that some ULTRA decrypts were available as early as 1939 and played a key role in persuading Churchill to order the withdrawal from France in June 1940. ULTRA also had a part to play in the story that will unfold in subsequent chapters – but not necessarily for the good.

Alongside GC&CS, there was also the establishment of what was known as Military Intelligence Branch 19 (MI19). This was an off-shoot of MI9, another Intelligence branch that dealt exclusively with Allied 'escape and evasion' methods, as well as obtaining valuable information from Allied prisoners who found themselves in Germany or Italy and had either escaped or been repatriated. According to M.R.D. Foot and J.M. Langley in their excellent account, *MI9 Escape and Evasion 1939–1945*, MI9 was a revamped Intelligence branch which had its roots in the First World War. Then known as MI1a, the organisation was involved in trying to obtain coded information from Allied prisoners incarcerated in Germany, but with little success. As war again loomed in 1938–9, MI1 was, like the Intelligence Corps, re-formed. This was initially on an ad hoc basis during the Munich Crisis and then permanently in 1939. On 23 December 1939, and with the tacit agreement of the War Office and other MI branches, especially MI5 and MI6, MI9 was officially recognised.[4]

Command of MI9 was given to Major Norman Crockatt DSO, MC, who had seen distinguished service in France in the First World War where he had been badly wounded. Although staying on in the Army after the war, Crockatt had become so disillusioned with peacetime soldiering that in 1927 he walked out of a Staff College lecture and resigned his commission. Perhaps more importantly, as is so often the case, Crockatt and the Director of Military Intelligence, Major-General Beaumont-Nesbitt, had known each other for some thirty years.[5] As Crockatt got to work organising his new department, it became very apparent that POW matters fell into two distinct halves: 'ours' and 'theirs'. If MI9 was to obtain information from Allied POWs, or organise their successful escapes, it had to know in as much detail as possible, the conditions under which its operatives would need to work. Consequently, Crockatt put his deputy, Major A.R. Rawlinson, another First World War MI1 old hand, in charge of enemy POW Intelligence, known soon after as MI9a. Rawlinson, a Royal Engineer on commissioning, had been remobilised in August 1939 as a captain. On taking up his new appointment, he found that he also had operational command over the Combined Services Detailed Interrogation Centre (CSDIC).

CSDIC was the main centre for deep interrogation of captured enemy personnel whom, it was thought, might know detailed information of a long-term operational or strategic nature. On the outbreak of war, CSDIC was located in the Tower of London but was moved soon after to Cockfosters Camp in Barnet, north

London. At this stage in the war, prisoners were few, mostly comprising German *Kriegsmarine* or *Luftwaffe* personnel, but as 1940 progressed, the number of prisoners rose. In 1942 CSDIC moved for the last time to Latimer and Beaconsfield, in Buckinghamshire.[6]

On general mobilisation, the problems of manpower were also addressed. The defunct Intelligence Corps was resurrected in early July 1940, becoming operational in December of the same year, under command of the Military Intelligence Directorate for selection and training of field officers and men. Those selected underwent basic military training before attending a series of courses at the new Intelligence Training Centre at Matlock, specialising in such fields as security, photographic interpretation and prisoner interrogation.[7]

In France, prior to the German attack, the BEF command Intelligence staffs were able to use what little time they had and actually analyse what they required from any potential prisoners, now that some form of unified, cooperating intelligence structure was in place in Whitehall. It was for this reason that Major Scotland was summoned. Although Major Scotland's stay in France seemed all too brief, he had set in motion a system for dealing with the administration of interrogating prisoners of war that has remained, virtually unchanged, to this day. In a post-operational report written in 1948 and now held in the Public Record Office at Kew, Scotland briefly described his role within the prisoner chain:

> In early 1940 the General Staff with the British Expeditionary Force (BEF) realised that, between the field interrogation by Unit Interrogators and Combined Services Detailed Interrogation Centre (CSDIC) in London, there was no method of obtaining higher grade interrogation [of POWs] then in existence.
>
> In March 1940 steps were taken to survey the possible sites for a GHQ Interrogation Unit and it was finally decided to site . . . a centre in conjunction with [POW] Camp No. 1, at Dieppe.
>
> After Dunkirk the need for a complete Field Intelligence Unit to provide 'I' [intelligence] cover for the United Kingdom defence troops was realised and PWIS(H), consisting of twenty officers with liberal transport, was formed on a War Establishment dated 13th July, 1940.[8]

PWIS(H) – Prisoner of War Interrogation Service (Home) – was to become Alexander Scotland's 'baby'. PWIS(H) was to hold the majority of POW interrogators who would be stationed throughout the country and undertake the detailed screening of prisoners for selection of onward movement to CSDIC. Scotland's report again:

> During this period the twenty interrogators in this unit were spread over the whole United Kingdom, where in each Command an Interrogation Centre was set up, provided with newly designed listening sets.
>
> German and Italian POWs were landed at many points within the United Kingdom throughout the war, when the cage [initial holding camp] nearest to the landing point was used to hold the POWs for investigation. At these cages prisoners were also selected for further treatment by CSDIC.[9]

Apart from covering the UK, PWIS(H) interrogators also went on some of the early raids against enemy coastal positions, especially in the Lofoten Islands, Vaagso, and St Nazaire. In the last example, the PWIS(H) officer was himself captured but managed to keep his true role from his captors until his release in 1945.

★ ★ ★

After the disastrous Battle of France and the evacuation from Dunkirk and other French Channel ports, Army Intelligence was able to consider seriously its position regarding the use of POWs for Intelligence purposes. While the RAF and Air Force Intelligence battled the *Luftwaffe* in the skies over southern England, Scotland and his staff at PWIS(H) drew up plans for dealing with POWs in the event of an invasion. Although the peripheral details were to be altered in 1944 prior to the Normandy landings, the core of the plan remained unchanged. For Scotland, the priority was that captured enemy personnel should be removed to the level of interrogation – tactical, operational or strategic – the individual prisoner warranted as soon as possible. To achieve the required speed, there had to be highly competent questioners further down the chain assessing each individual's potential. Scotland and his planners envisaged a five-tier system starting at the point of capture. This is worth looking at in detail.

The capturing unit was to collect all prisoners, disarm them and gather any documentation, maps and other paperwork. Prisoners would then be moved to the Unit Collecting Point, normally just behind the front lines and manned by echelon troops of the same unit. Here also the unit intelligence officers (IOs) would identify prisoners by name, rank and unit, at the same time questioning them for any tactical information. This was to be done as soon as possible, not only to maintain the 'shock of capture', but also to release the guarding manpower that such a system entailed. If a unit was unable to conduct the questioning itself, then the prisoner could be moved further back to a Brigade Regulating Point where tactical questioning could also be conducted. From the units or brigades, POWs would then be moved back again to the Divisional Cage. Here, they would be handed over to the Divisional Provost Staff – military policemen – and the divisional intelligence staffs would confirm any details already obtained or, if not already undertaken, conduct tactical questioning. Another important feature of the Divisional Cage involved the break-down of any prisoner cohesion by enforcing strict separation by rank. With the obvious leaders removed, the 'shock of capture' among the rank and file could be maintained. In the autumn of 1940, Divisional Cages in the south of the country were located at Horndean in Hampshire (4th Division), Okehampton in Devon (48th Division) and Blandford in Dorset (50th Division). Strict rules were laid down for these cages. War Office regulations for 'The Orders for the Disposal of Prisoners of War captured in Great Britain', described these cages:

> . . . barbed wire enclosures of a simple type, capable of holding 250 men. Officers and other ranks must be kept in separate enclosures. Separate pens must be provided for those awaiting interrogation.

From the Divisional Cages, prisoners were dispatched by the quickest possible means to the Command Cages which, in the case of the south of England (Southern Command) were located in Swindon and Aylesbury. Here prisoners would be seen for the first time by MI9a (later MI19) PWIS(H) staff who would also evaluate the prisoners. They were looking for any individuals who might be expected to hold detailed information of an operational or strategic nature, warranting long-term and detailed interrogation. It was deemed necessary that the Command Cages should not hold prisoners for longer than forty-eight hours while selections took place, thus regulating them to the role of a transit camp. From here prisoners would either be moved to the CSDIC Cage at Cockfosters, known for security reasons as POW Camp 10, or, in urgent cases, would stay in the Command Cage itself for detailed interrogation. Here also, segregation was intensified, for those prisoners worthy of further interrogation were now separated from each other, further creating the sense of isolation. In turn, those prisoners not required for further questioning would come under War Office authority and be dispatched to War Office POW camps. These camps were administered by the First Directorate of the Department for Prisoners of War (PW1).[10]

While the plans for coping with POWs were being organised, Scotland and the PWIS(H), alongside MI9a, also thought about the techniques they would employ for the interrogations. It should be noted here, that such areas were, and thankfully still are, heavily regulated by the Geneva Convention. At no time were interrogators permitted to use physical violence on a prisoner and there are no incidents recorded in the archives to suggest that detailed interrogators ever did. In fact, due to the maintenance of the 'shock of capture', interrogators often found themselves trying to quieten down prisoners, especially Italians, as they spilled everything. At the end of the war, it was discovered that Germany did not run general courses on counter-interrogation techniques as MI9 did. Rather akin to the Soviet mentality, soldiers were not expected to surrender!

An interesting description of CSDIC in the latter half of the war was given by Colonel L. St Clare Grondona who was placed in command after the centre moved to Wilton Park just outside Beaconsfield:

Our troops' hutments were spaced amid tall trees within a few hundred yards of a Georgian mansion – the White House – which was our Officers' Mess. The prisoners' compound, with its four long intersecting corridors leading to brick-and-cement cells had been built within a 14 ft brick wall that had enclosed a two-acre vegetable garden and orchard, and its low roofs were so camouflaged as to merge into the surrounding landscape. . . . Cells were centrally heated and each had ample space for four spring-mattressed beds. There were no bars across the windows, but the several small panes in each were set in steel frames that would have baffled Houdini.

In the early stages of the war all our prisoners were survivors from either shot-down aircraft or destroyed submarines. They were a tough lot, cockily confident that it was only a matter of time before Hitler had complete control of Europe and had crushed Britain. . . . But many of these men possessed valuable information, and it was our job to extract from them as much as possible of this – always with proper regard to the Geneva Convention.

So it was that our interrogating officers had to be wily and resourceful. Our methods of interrogation were processes of painless extraction, and more often than not a 'guest' was unaware that he had given us any useful information.

All interrogation officers spoke fluent German. Most of them had spent much time in Nazi Germany, perhaps as students or in business, and knew a great deal more about the real Hitler than did most of our prisoners. The opening gambit was likely to take the form of a discussion which bore no resemblance to an interrogation. Its first phase might be to sow doubts in a prisoner's mind about propaganda that had been fed to him over the years.[11]

There were three methods used by the British and their Allies for obtaining information from prisoners. The first involved direct questioning. This was often the best way, especially so if the prisoner was judged to be cooperative. Quite often, Scotland and his men found many German soldiers opposed to the Nazi ideology, especially towards the end of the war, and all too willing to cooperate. This yielded much valuable information and allowed CSDIC to put together a veritable library of information that was used against others not so keen. This worked very well and harder prisoners often gave up when faced with a barrage of detailed information about themselves, their superiors and their units. What was the point of resisting if the questioner appeared to know everything already? For such a system to work, however, the onus was very much on the interrogator. He had to have a detailed understanding of the mentality of the prisoner he was dealing with, something Scotland was all too aware of and had advocated from the very beginning.

The second method of gleaning information was through the use of concealed microphones. Initially very bulky instruments, these were concealed in the walls and ceilings of individual cells at

Cockfosters and the London Cage. Prisoners found themselves temporarily held with one or two others, normally under the pretext of over-crowding in the camp. All conversations would then be monitored and copied down by staff detailed to listen in. On occasions this proved highly successful. Perhaps the best known example was that involving the German Generals von Thoma, who had been briefly in command of the Afrika Korps prior to his capture by an officer of the 10th Hussars in March 1943, and Cruewell, also from the Afrika Korps. They were temporarily held at the London Cage, which was also Scotland's headquarters for PWIS(H), and were put into the same cell. Unbeknown to them, the cell was fixed with microphones. Richard Garrett in his work *P.O.W.* wrote:

> Once they had exchanged the customary greetings, one of them was overheard to remark that he was surprised to find London in such good shape. He had expected it to be more or less razed to the ground. His companion asked him why. The general then went on to talk about an unmanned machine of fearful potential that he had seen under test at some highly secret firing range in Germany.

Of course the two Generals were talking about the V1 flying bomb, something that British Intelligence had little knowledge of at the time. Garrett continued:

> It was only after the conversation between Generals Thoma and Cruewell that MI6 applied itself to a more thorough investigation of the matter. As General Ismay noted in a memorandum to Winston Churchill, their talk indicated 'a foundation of fact even if the details are inaccurate'.[12]

The third and final method that was adopted involved the use of 'stool pigeons'. This was very risky and the introduction of the 'pigeon' had to be very carefully planned, especially as regarded the 'character' that was to be adopted. Moreover, the 'pigeon' was under considerable strain, especially as such individuals were recruited from the large German refugee population that had arrived before the war. By 1940 there had been only four such recruits, while at the close of hostilities in Europe in May 1945, only a total of forty-nine had been selected and trained, including some former POWs.[13]

Apart from the standard POW interrogations, Scotland's PWIS(H) also investigated any attempted escapes from the camps. Although these were numerous, the escapees normally found themselves ill-equipped to last more than a few days in the countryside. The majority of Germans had little or no English and found it very difficult to find their way about a countryside devoid of signposts. These had all been removed as an anti-invasion measure in 1940. Escapers who did reach the coast then had to cross either the Irish Sea to southern Ireland (and further internment), or the Channel to occupied Europe. None are recorded as having succeeded, although some notable escapes were made from POW camps in Canada, Kenya and India.

With PWIS(H) and CSDIC firmly established by the late summer of 1940, prisoners from as far afield as North Africa began to arrive in Britain. Most were senior officers or technicians who required detailed, intensive interrogation, especially as regards new enemy weapon technology. For the ordinary soldiers captured in North Africa, both Italians and later Germans, Middle East Command had established its own detailed questioning centre close to GHQ in Cairo, known as CSDIC(ME). This centre was open by December 1940 and could accommodate some sixty prisoners at any one time.[14]

In 1942, after the Japanese entry into the war in the Far East, South East Asia Command also required its own centre and CSDIC(India) was opened, based at the Red Fort in Delhi. CSDIC(I) differed slightly from the others in that it had a separate section, 'Z Section', based at Cranwich Camp in Norfolk. The thinking behind this was that there were many Indian Army troops fighting in North Africa and later Italy. At the same time, Germany was attempting to raise an 'Indian Legion' of its own from disaffected Indian officers and other ranks, headed by the nationalist leader Chandra Bose. Although over three thousand former Indian Army soldiers did join up, they saw little combat, stationed as they were on the Biscay coast in southern France. After D-Day in June 1944, and more importantly the landings on the southern French coast in August of the same year, the 'Indian Legion' was withdrawn back to Germany. On the way it clashed with both the American 3rd and 7th Armies, as well as the French Resistance. It was during this withdrawal that many of its men were captured or just simply deserted.

Apart from dealing with POWs, Scotland and his team also had to screen the many refugees who came to Britain, escaping from the German-occupied countries. In his report, Scotland summed up this task as follows:

When, in early 1941, MI9 accepted the responsibility for the interrogation of friendly aliens arriving from enemy and enemy-occupied territory, PWIS(H) lent officers to organise and initiate the work. Even when an establishment was provided for [the formation of] MI19 . . . PWIS(H) officers continued to help as interrogators until the former unit was disbanded on 31 May 45.[15]

By 1944 therefore the organisation for dealing with prisoners of war was fully integrated into the overall intelligence community. Lessons were still being learned, however. On the final surrender in North Africa, nigh on some 250,000 enemy personnel of all services were captured. Never before had the Allies had to deal with such vast numbers of prisoners, despite the experience of the large numbers of Italians who fell into Allied hands in 1941. The majority of these prisoners were either held in Egypt or shipped to Canada and America. This was possible as there was some breathing space between the final collapse in Tunisia and the main landings in Italy. For the Normandy landings, however, the system would rely on POWs being quickly returned to the United Kingdom, both to remove them from the initial battle areas (as dictated by the Geneva Convention), as well as to be able to extract any vital intelligence regarding the 'Second Front' campaign. Somehow, the efficiency of the system had to be maintained. Several measures were put into place, as Scotland described:

Other duties were then added. The MP [Military Police] personnel detailed for the duty of escorting and guarding POWs of the Liberation Armies received technical instruction from PWIS(H) officers.

The American teams of Intelligence personnel all received practical training in 1944 by serving together with PWIS(H) officers.

The invasion of France was expected to produce large numbers of POWs and the method of transportation and treatment on arrival here called for an increase in PWIS(H) strength. Authority was obtained in two stages, ultimately bringing the strength of the unit to 29 officers and 35 sergeants, all German speakers.

This increase was proved to be necessary for, in addition to the normal operation of obtaining military information from POWs of all enemy sources, the sorting and classification of the men was an arduous task, as the numbers eventually ran into hundreds of thousands.[16]

By 'classification', Scotland was referring to the newly introduced system of classifying the political nature of each German prisoner. This was a simple process of grading each man as 'White', 'Grey' or 'Black'. 'Whites' were those judged to be 'anti-Nazi' and who might be persuaded to work actively for the Allies, either in the camps themselves or in such diverse tasks as broadcasting to Germany or those countries still occupied. The 'Greys' were those POWs who showed themselves not to have any particular political allegiance but were thought unlikely to work for the Allies. 'Blacks', however, were those prisoners who showed true loyalty to Hitler and National Socialism during their initial screenings. These prisoners would have to be watched very carefully and on the whole, most were sent to Canada or America. Some, however, remained in the United Kingdom.

As PWIS(H) expanded, so did the number of POW camps up and down the country. The main camps were to be found in a variety of locations, from former textile mills such as those at Warth Mills in Bury and Glen Mill in Oldham, to former hutted Army barracks such as Le Marchant Camp in Devizes, Wiltshire. Some, such as that at Comrie in Perthshire, Scotland, were purpose-built by Pioneer Corps companies. Several of them were designated 'Transit' camps and their task was to conduct the initial administration of prisoners once they had been transported inland from the port of landing, usually by train.

PWIS(H) also needed to expand its range of screening centres to cope with the likely influx of prisoners. Consequently, a reception camp was opened at the Kempton Park racecourse, which was ideal for the purpose owing to its large open spaces. Here Scotland's men would screen POWs for onward movement to CSDIC while other Naval or Air Force Intelligence personnel would hunt for sources of technical information. Any prisoner not required at CSDIC but thought to be a potential source of special information as outlined in briefs received by PWIS(H) from the Field Armies or the War

Office, would be moved to either the Lingfield, Kempton or London Cages. These three specialist camps would become very important when the war was over and PWIS(H) became the War Crimes Investigation Unit (WCIU) in December 1945.

Doug Richards was posted to the WCIU at the London Cage in 1945. A member of the Welsh Guards based at Sandown Park, Esher, he had been called into his Company Sergeant Major's office and asked if he could speak German. He answered 'No', and was promptly told to learn some in four hours. He had been posted to London. The next day Doug duly arrived at 6 and 8 Kensington Palace Gardens where he was interviewed by Scotland himself. Passing muster, he was instructed to sign up to the Official Secrets Act and thence started work. Doug Richards recalls:

The duties laid out were for internal security and the conveying of the POWs between locations as required. For this I was also issued a Smith & Wesson .38 pistol and ammo as well as being given retraining on it.

I was then introduced to the staff, all very informal. We were each called by our Christian names as no surnames were allowed whilst within earshot of the prisoners.

Nos 6 and 8 Kensington Palace Gardens were rather imposing mansions, both situated next door to the Russian Embassy [in No. 7]. The main office and interrogation rooms were in No. 6, while the basement of No. 8 housed the kitchens and dining areas for the staff. On the ground floor were the reception rooms and guard room for the perimeter guards (independent to the Cage). On the first floor, all the bedrooms had been converted to secure rooms for the detention of those being investigated. Each room, or cell, had a small table, a single camp-type bed and a chair.

The general routine was that one of the interrogation officers would request to see a specific prisoner. The latter would then be escorted to No. 6. Each escort was expected to sit in during the questioning and then return the prisoner to his room. Often the prisoners were given paper and pencils to write down aspects of his war movements – countries, towns and so on.[17]

Internal duties were not all Doug Richards was expected to carry out. He also had to convey the secret reports produced through the interrogations:

I also had to carry Top Secret papers for distribution to MI9 and the

Americans. These were strapped under my shirt. I personally made the journey from the Cage to a building in Bond Street, a distance of some 4 to 5 miles, as well as to SHAEF Headquarters in Grosvenor Square, again about 4 miles. I was not allowed to use public transport under any circumstances and had to walk each time.

One day, whilst escorting Field Marshal Kesselring, he asked me if he could be shown how to highly polish shoes. This was to relieve his boredom. I instructed him and supplied my own shoes, with polish and a duster. He also asked me if I could take a letter to his sister. I was astonished at this request and I took him to mean when I next went to Germany. But no, his sister lived in Holland Park, not far from the Cage.

I took the letter to Colonel Scotland who himself did not know this. He read the letter and then told me to go if I so wished. It transpired that the sister was a naturalised British subject married to a British Army officer. The letter was just a request for some decent soap and razor blades. Of course, these were not given to him!

Of Colonel Scotland, Doug Richards had this to say:

Lieutenant Colonel Scotland – 'The Boss' as he was known – was really a pure civilian through and through. We Guardsmen stood head and shoulders over him, but he never looked up to a tall person. He was always quiet-mannered but when a prisoner tried to make a fool of him, he really exploded. We had some very nasty people among the prisoners and they were treated accordingly. No one was above reproach and the prisoners knew that once they were sent for, the end was near.[18]

Given the proximity to the Soviet Embassy, security was particularly tight after the war. Doug Richards again:

A party of White Russians arrived at the London Cage in early 1946. The Russian Embassy duly ordered its security men to stand in the middle of the road armed with machine guns. We were then asked to hand over the prisoners. When we asked the Russians why, they replied, 'We shoot them now . . .'. How the Russians knew of the arrival of the prisoners we never found out.[19]

CHAPTER THREE

Devizes and the Military

The barrack-square, washed clean with rain,
Shines wet and wintry-grey and cold.

Siegfried Sassoon (1918)[1]

To those who know Devizes, the small, rural, Wiltshire market town epitomises the southern English countryside. Embellished with a rich history, it is believed locally that the town's origins date back as far as 400 BC when King Dunwallo is said to have founded an early settlement there. Roman artefacts are often unearthed during major building programmes; one of the better discoveries was a Romano-British cemetery found in 1960 when a new local school at Southbroom was built.

The town's link with prisoners can also be traced back a very long way. Bishop Osmund, at the beginning of the twelfth century, is recorded as having built a wooden castle with motte and bailey here. Within its walls, Robert, Duke of Normandy, the eldest son of William the Conqueror, was incarcerated by his brother King Henry. Eventually, it is recorded, this wooden castle was destroyed by fire and in its place Bishop Roger of Salisbury built a stone replacement. Devizes was the largest of three such castles and was apparently the most magnificent, with a 'military aspect said to be the most important fortress in the west of England'.[2] It was due to the presence of Bishop Roger's castle that the town was established.

During the Middle Ages, a flourishing wool trade grew up, bringing wealth to the area. By the fifteenth century Devizes rivalled Salisbury in its manufacturing of cloth and was well known for its 'Vyze blankets'. With the wealth came the establishment of a weekly market, thought to date back to 1228 but certainly regularly recorded from 1609 onwards. This was normally a Thursday market, as it still is today.

Battle first came to Devizes during the Civil War when the loyalties of the town were divided. The town's mayor, Richard Pierce, held for the King while the two local Members of Parliament, Sir Edward Baynton and Robert Nicholas, were both firmly for Cromwell and his Roundheads. In 1643 the conflicting loyalties were brought to a head when Devizes was besieged by Sir William Waller, who was determined to defeat Prince Maurice and Sir Ralph Hopton, firmly holed up in Devizes Castle. Siege guns were deployed by the Roundheads: the tower of St James's Church still shows signs of damage. Running short of supplies, including musket matches and lead for shot, the Royalists sallied forth from Devizes on 13 July 1644. In a swift battle, now known as the Battle of Roundway, Hopton's Cavaliers saw off the King's enemies with much bloodshed as the latter fled the field on foot, only to be cut down as they ran.

Cromwell never forgave Devizes. A year later his troops once again besieged the town, but with far greater forces. When the Royalist powder magazine was hit, the Royalists were forced to raise a white flag. In anger, Cromwell ordered the destruction of what remained of Bishop Roger's fortress. But the names of Prince Maurice, Waller and Hopton were not forgotten. In 1939–40, when three new militia barracks were built nearby, they were named after the former protagonists.

After the Civil War, Devizes continued to grow as a wealthy market town. Cloth continued to be important, as did the grinding of snuff and the brewing of beer. The military was never far away, with the then Lieutenant-Colonel James Wolfe reputedly spending five weeks in the town recruiting. Three years later he was dead, forever to be known as 'General Wolfe, the Hero of Quebec'.

By the middle of the nineteenth century, the prosperity of the town warranted the opening of a railway, a single-track branch line. This line took eleven years to build and was an expensive venture. Devizes lies some 400 ft above sea level, so the line required extensive engineering work, just as the Kennet and Avon canal before it had done. A long tunnel was dug on the approach from the east, which ran for some 190 yards under the castle mound; the tunnel foundations were sunk some 30 ft down to the bedrock. In the process many interesting artefacts were discovered from the old castle. The work was eventually completed and on 1 July 1857, the line was declared open, amid much excitement. As the railway companies expanded their networks throughout the country, so the Devizes line became the major transportation method for heavy goods to and from the town. With considerable foresight, the Great Western Railway Company, which owned the line, had bought up the canal company, thus securing a virtual local transport monopoly. The railway continued to maintain its new-found position as the foremost mode of transport until after the Second World War when there was greater dependence on the road network. Indeed, between 1939 and 1945, the station and its large goods yard was probably at its busiest.[3]

Although Devizes and its old town hall had been the administrative headquarters for the Wiltshire Militia since the Act of 1757, it was not until 1859 and as a direct result of the Crimean War, that the military came to reside in the town in any great numbers. In 1854 there had been a recruiting drive in the town. The influx of volunteers was so great that the famous Bear Inn had to be taken over as a local headquarters with Coldstream Guards NCOs handling the basic drilling. It appears that the enthusiasm shown by the volunteers, mostly shepherds and farm workers who had travelled long distances to answer the call to arms, encouraged the War Office to build a barracks on the Bath Road, the first in Devizes.[4] Although very little information remains today, the Bath Road Barracks was dwarfed by an even larger complex in 1878, built at the opposite end of the town on the London Road. This was named Le Marchant Barracks after the famous Colonel Sir Gaspard Le Marchant, once commander of the 99th Foot, which later became the Second Battalion, the Wiltshire Regiment. The building of such a large complex was a direct result of the 1873 Cardwell Reforms. As Minister for War, Lord Cardwell passed through Parliament his Localisation Scheme whereby all county formations were to come under a new District Commander with a local depot. Devizes was chosen for the Wiltshire Regiment. Consequently, both the 62nd and 99th Regiments of Foot, as well as the local militia, now relied on Devizes as their central recruiting and training base. Land adjacent to the London Road was bought from the government's Woods and Forests Department for some £3,000. Work commenced immediately.

Further reforms in 1881, when all militia units became battalions in their own right, and 1908, when all volunteer units became part of a territorial force, saw much greater activity at Le Marchant Barracks. Whenever the parent battalions went overseas, they normally left behind a Depot Company to ensure an efficient administrative link with the home town. The Depot was also the initial basic training centre for the Regiment, prior to recruits moving on to further, more specific training at a Brigade Depot. In the case of the Wiltshire Regiment, this was the Wessex Brigade Depot at Topsham Barracks in Exeter. In the 1960s a series of government cuts not only axed all Regimental training centres, but also forced the amalgamation of many of the famous county regiments. The Wiltshire Regiment was no exception, and was amalgamated with the Royal Berkshires. Although the new Regiment's depot was located in Exeter, alongside its training centre, one of the Territorial battalions remained in Le Marchant Barracks, thus maintaining the long link between Devizes and the military.[5]

During the First World War, Devizes was very active in the support of its own Regiment. Huge recruiting drives, especially that by Lord Kitchener, ensured that Le Marchant Barracks was full of new recruits undergoing their basic training. The redundant Kennet and Avon canal was also used for instructional purposes by troops designated to become barge operators in France and Flanders. At the same time, the call to arms throughout the Empire saw Canadian soldiers in the town for the first time in 1914. These soldiers would fight at the Second Battle of Ypres and would be the first to encounter the use of poison gas on a battlefield.[6]

The outbreak of the Second World War saw the greatest expansion of the military life in Devizes. The urgent need for manpower to rebuild the British Armed Forces after the stagnation during the inter-war years saw Le Marchant Barracks at full capacity again. All four of the Wiltshire Regiment's battalions were called up and marched through Le Marchant Barracks alongside some reservists of the Welch Regiment, thus necessitating the formation of a regimental training centre and the construction of extra accommodation for all the reservists once again called to the colours. Land was set aside adjacent to the barracks where, to begin with, soldiers were billeted under canvas. This new camp was called 'Le Marchant Camp' and was really an extension of the old brick-built barracks. Further camp accommodation was deemed necessary as a direct result of the Conscription Act, which called up every able-bodied man under the age of thirty-five. And so, during the spring of 1939, the first foundations were laid for three new barrack complexes. Called Hopton, Waller and Prince Maurice Barracks, they were situated opposite Le Marchant Barracks and were initially referred to as the Militia Camps. The contract was given to the local firm Chivers and the first of some 2,200 militiamen arrived in July of the same year.[7]

This upsurge in military activity throughout the town did not go unreported. The Wiltshire Regiment Journal Depot Notes of June 1939 made these comments:

These notes go to press on the eve of what promises to be a very busy period for the Depot – it will certainly upset the tranquil atmosphere of Devizes. After receiving the first batch of Reservists who are being called up for temporary service with the Depot and 2nd Battalion, we shall be preparing for the 'advent' of the Militia, to allow for which the regular Recruit Company will be 'lent' to the 2nd Battalion for two months. At the end of this period, huts will be ready to accommodate both the Regular and Militia Recruits . . .

We are to have more troops as neighbours, as the new Camps just over the road from the Barracks are already taking shape and the AAs [Anti Aircraft – in fact the 207th Training Regiment] and SLs [Search Lights] will soon be in occupation. This should help things considerably in the way of sport, and a little military competition will be very welcome, as I'm sure we have been left to ourselves here far too long.[8]

To emphasise the importance of the new camps, Lord Gort VC, the future commander of the British Expeditionary Force in France, visited the new site on 10 August 1939, and described the spirit of those soldiers he met as 'amazingly good'. This might have been a trifle surprising to those in the know, since all contemporary photographs show a sea of mud and 150 recruits had recently been complaining about the over-abundance of tinned salmon in the daily rations.[9]

Alongside the soldiers, the raising of the Women's Auxiliary Territorial Service (the ATS) also went ahead, with the 40th

Wiltshire Company affiliated to the Wiltshire Regiment Depot. The Regimental Journal had this to say:

> Its members have already attended for a couple of evenings for instruction in their duties at the Orderly Room, Quartermaster's Office and Stores, and the Cookhouse, and there is no doubt that they are very eager to learn. They are due to come here for a week's 'In Camp Training' next month – practise in 'counting ten before speaking one's mind' has, I hear, already commenced to ensure that the complete military vocabulary at least may be retained as a heritage by the mere men of the Army.[10]

Pauline Parker was a member of the ATS in Devizes and has a vivid memory of those first days:

> My strongest memory of those times is of being drilled by a drill-sergeant of the Coldstream Guards. He had never trained girls before and considered the job very much beneath his dignity. Also, I believe, he was being teased by his fellow sergeants in the mess, because he greeted us on our first day with 'I don't intend being made a laughing stock by a bunch of **** girls, so watch it!' He reduced some of the girls to tears and we all got blisters, but before long we found ourselves enjoying it . . . at the end of the course the sergeant had the grace to say he had never had a squad of men who had learned more quickly or become smarter than we had, and he was proud of us.[11]

As the BEF battled tenaciously to extract itself from the Dunkirk beaches, the call went out on 14 May 1940 from Anthony Eden, then Secretary of State for War, for the formation of the Local Defence Volunteers (LDV), later known as the Home Guard. Today, the Home Guard is regarded as something to smile, even sneer at. In the summer of 1940, it was anything but that. The county of Wiltshire raised its fair share of Home Guard Battalions, thirteen in all, with an additional AA Rocket Battery and Motor Transport Company to boot. The Devizes and Trowbridge volunteers were under the command of the second Lord Roundway, Edward Murray Colston, of Roundway Park. A former Grenadier Guards officer, he had seen action in both the Boer War and the First World War, in which he won the DSO. Now holding the rank of Brigadier-General for the duration, he helped form the 4th Battalion, Wiltshire Home Guard, and by 28 May 1940 some 1,200 able-bodied men had come forward. On 2 July, the figure had risen to 2,609 and by the spring of 1941 reached a ceiling of 2,629.[12] The Devizes Company of the Battalion, some 366 strong, was based at the Liberal Club, close to the Town Hall. Initially very poorly equipped, mostly with shotguns, a few revolvers, 'Molotov Cocktails' made from a petrol and creosote mixture, and home-made pikestaffs, the Home Guard would have been very hard pressed had they met any well-equipped German paratroopers, as was the fear.

Arthur Cleverly was just seventeen years old in May 1940, but remembers the day he joined the LDV:

> I was then seventeen and eagerly went to register at the police station. At the first meeting held at the Scout Hall, we discovered that most of the recruits were veterans from the Great War. We were sworn in and issued with our 'uniforms', a black armband with the letters LDV, or as some wags dubbed it 'Look, Duck and Vanish'. I was put into number 1 Platoon and our post was in the old summerhouse at the back of the Rotherstone allotments.
>
> We had a fearsome collection of weapons – 12-bore shotguns, .22 rifles and .45 revolvers. I managed to acquire a Winchester .45 rifle and ammunition from a retired gamekeeper. It had a kick like a mule. In the evenings we did shooting practice, firing air rifles at tins. Some men even had kitchen knives which were ground down until they were razor sharp.
>
> Soon the LDV became the Home Guard. We were given our uniform with the badge of the Wiltshire Regiment and were issued with American P17 .300 rifles. We now practised on proper rifle ranges but somehow the early magic had gone.[13]

John Perkins was also a member of the 4th Battalion, although he did not join up until early 1941, after his sixteenth birthday:

> Once I was sixteen, I joined D Company of the 4th Battalion. I was posted to the Anti-Tank platoon where we had a two-pounder we used to pull around the town. We were based at the old Devizes Drill Hall, now the TA Centre Club.
>
> Sometimes, we used to be sent to guard the railway station which also had a petrol store. God, dear-oh-dear, how we did it, I don't know. Guarding all night and then back for milking at 6.00 a.m.
>
> We also used to do guard duties in the pillboxes. For this we had an old .300 rifle, six rounds of ammunition and a bayonet. Every weekend we

had training, done by a sergeant in the East Lancashires. If you didn't turn up you were prosecuted. We used to do it on the playing fields of Southbroom School . . . morale was always very high though.[14]

The realities of war came to Devizes in June 1940 with the arrival of some of the survivors of Dunkirk. Every possible space in the south of England was used to accommodate those who had made it back across the Channel. Devizes was no exception. In his book about the Devizes Railway, Nigel Bray was to write:

One of the saddest sights was that of trainloads of British troops – many of them wet through, others heavily bandaged – arriving at Devizes direct from the beaches after the evacuation of Dunkirk.[15]

Terry Gaylard, a local journalist and historian, also remembered the sad sight and some forty years later wrote in the *Wiltshire Gazette*, 'They presented a dishevelled, pitiful sight as they wandered around the town, lucky to be alive'.[16] Another eye-witness was Mrs Hehir, who in 1939 had joined the ATS, much to her husband's disapproval. Having survived the rigours of the drill square, she found herself working in the Quartermaster's department as the Dunkirk survivors came through:

I was called up for ATS Local Service training in 1939 and was there when those from France came through. I worked in the Quartermaster's store and will always remember those boys . . . we just handed them everything they wanted. We didn't bother to look at the sizes, just handed them out. They were so tired and dirty but never grumbled. I will always remember how polite they were to us.[17]

Many of the locals still alive today claim that upwards of some 35,000 Dunkirk evacuees were brought through Devizes. 'Although the camps . . . were extensive, they could not cope with the numbers, and men were sleeping on the ground. . . . Some of them wandered about the town or sat on the pavements, and soon a canteen was opened for them.'[18]

But for a few of those who arrived at Devizes in those forlorn days of 1940, life was not all bad. Members of the 2nd Battalion, the Wiltshire Regiment, including the remnants of the band, were especially well looked after, having suffered a particular mauling outside Dunkirk. Dr Ian Samuel had also been in France with the 6th Field Ambulance. Hit by flying debris when the French blew up a bridge, Ian Samuel made it to the mole at Malo-les-Bains on 29 May from where he was eventually evacuated in a Dutch vessel and ferried to Margate. From there he boarded a train at Ramsgate and arrived at Addison Road Station in London:

> Now Addison Road Station is, or was, the only point in the British rail system that could distribute a train to any main line throughout the whole of Britain . . . we, of course, had no idea where we were going, but as the journey wore on and it got darker the Colonel asked me if I had any idea of which direction we were going. I said I hadn't, but he said – looking out of the window – 'I've got a feeling we're in Wiltshire'. This seemed very optimistic to me. However, a little later he said 'I think we're getting to my home town of Devizes', and this surprised me even more. His confidence was supreme. Within a quarter of an hour the train pulled up at a station and I looked out of the window. The notice on the platform said 'Devizes' and, as if this wasn't enough, there on the platform was his wife!
>
> She had heard that there were some troops coming from Dunkirk to Devizes Station and just on the off-chance that out of all those thousands of men who were being evacuated one would be her husband, she had come to Devizes Station. Everybody of course saw them, for he was 6' 7" and she was 6' 1".

Ian Samuel went on to record how those at Le Marchant Barracks looked after them so magnificently:

> We went to the depot of the Royal Wiltshire Regiment who really laid out the red carpet for us. It was just about the middle of their weekly Mess Night and they made room for us, gave us a whopping great meal and their Commandant gave the order that the Officers should give up their beds for us . . . to give you some idea of my tiredness and exhaustion, I slept straight for 16 hours.[19]

Ian Samuel spent only four days at Devizes before he and his colonel rejoined the remnants of the Field Ambulance in Halifax, Yorkshire.

By the beginning of 1941, the immediate threat of a German invasion had diminished. Manpower targets had been met by the War Office through conscription, although the fighting in North Africa and later the sad losses in the Far East, meant that the demand for men, especially infantry, continued. In Devizes, the military had settled down to a routine of training and black-outs. No longer required as the Wiltshire Regiment Training Centre, Le Marchant Camp fell vacant except for passing units who were billeted there for short periods, as well as for multifarious stores units of the Royal Engineers and Royal Army Service Corps. Le Marchant Barracks was always full, however. Alongside the small Wiltshire Regiment Depot staff, there were various units that used the barracks for varying lengths of time including the 6th Battalion, the Wiltshire Regiment – a Home Defence Battalion – which was there until disbandment in 1943. They were followed by a variety of units including a Royal Artillery Field Regiment, a Royal Marine detachment and several others. Across the road Hopton, Prince Maurice and Waller Barracks were also in constant use. Another, smaller, complex was also built, and came to be known as 'Anzac' Camp. This was primarily used as ATS accommodation as no such facilities existed in the main brick buildings.

The Japanese attack on Pearl Harbor on 7 December 1941 ensured the entry of the United States into the war. With remarkable aplomb, Winston Churchill persuaded President Roosevelt that the greater threat lay in Hitler's conquered Europe and not in the Far East, despite the initial set-backs. Consequently, in June 1942 the country learnt that American troops and equipment would be arriving very soon and in huge numbers. These large forces would need accommodation, vehicle parks and training areas, preferably in the south of England, close to the Channel.

By the beginning of 1943, the United States Army had established itself around Salisbury Plain and adjacent areas. The garrisons at Tidworth, Perham Down and Warminster were handed over complete, including their schools and married quarters. Alongside these, a further eighteen camps were also available near to the Plain, as well as others not too far away. One of these latter locations was Devizes.[20]

Waller and Prince Maurice Barracks were the first two to be taken over in Devizes. Initially, the hutted camps were occupied by smaller American units, one of the first being the 344th Engineer Regiment. Soon, however, Devizes was to play host to units of a much larger formation, the American 4th Armored Division. Two of the front-line components of the Division arrived in Devizes at the end of January 1944, 37th Tank Battalion moving into Waller Barracks and the 22nd Armored Field Artillery Battalion into the Prince Maurice huts. Assorted other support units also moved in, with an American Transport Regiment eventually occupying Le Marchant Barracks, once the 6th Wiltshires had been disbanded.

This book is not the place to describe the American sojourn in Devizes. To some they were late in arriving, while to others they brought hope at last that Hitler could – and would – be defeated. For many of the Americans, Devizes and the unspoilt countryside were a wonder to behold, to others it was damp and dreary. Harry Feinberg served with the 37th Tank Battalion. Now living in New York, he recalled his first impressions:

Our 4th Armored Division docked at a port in Swansea, Wales, early in January 1944. I remember being a bit nervous that they kept us aboard ship for two days and nights, especially since we were told that the *Luftwaffe* had bombed there a few days earlier.

We disembarked the second night, were herded onto trains (unlike the trains of the US) [and] it seemed like a long ride to our destination. We were accounted for and herded again to our barracks. Very dingy, double-deck beds with extremely uncomfortable straw mattresses, drapes drawn to shade any light from escaping outdoors.

The camp was huge. We had our meals in the nearby mess hall, the motor pool was nearby and lots of time was spent with our vehicles, cleaning, driving, checking them out to make sure they were in the best of condition. These were the vehicles that we were going to use as our wheels and armament across the Channel, so they had to be in tip-top shape. For the personnel it was the same daily routines, such as guard duty, K.P. clean up, inspections, marching, callisthenics to keep us in shape, and more. I remember England as being damp and the evenings very dark.

I . . . remember Devizes itself. There was some sort of pond or lake [The Crammer] stocked with white swans and I remember one of them being very nasty, chasing any of the American GIs who walked past the water. I had never heard of the combination of fish and chips before and thought it odd that the product was placed in a cone made of newspaper. I personally preferred ice cream, but there was none available during war time. We visited the one movie theatre, the pubs and the dances that were held for us at our leisure hours.

During our manoeuvres we did get to see the beautiful English countryside, green dales and valleys, farms and haystacks, cattle. I also remember the thatched-roof homes in the area, something I had never seen before and I could not figure out how the thatch kept out the rain. Weren't the roofs vulnerable to fire in the summer when everything was so dry?[21]

The 1989 4th Armored Division Association Newsletter *Rolling Together* also mentioned wartime Devizes. Charles Waffle kept in touch with the family of Mrs Beryl Underwood, who befriended many Americans. When he discovered a letter in his attic that he had forgotten to post all those years ago, he wrote again; of the 1,500 members of his Division who lost their lives fighting the Germans in Europe he said:

Their last memories of peace on earth was of your little town, Devizes. How you put up with us Yanks, I'll never know. Maybe we got rowdy at times after a few drinks, having a good time and not knowing what the future held for us. Certainly all of us have fond memories of your town and its wonderful people.[22]

As a part of General Patton's Third Army, the 4th Armored also came in for its own fair share of inspections. Harry Feinberg again:

I remember us being alerted that a General Patton was coming into the camp and that we had to virtually scrub everything squeaky clean. We were told to disappear, stay out of sight, that this was an inspection tour. Some of the boys working in the mess hall did get to see 'His Highness' walk his way through. I'm told he had an entourage of military personnel accompanying him, along with newspaper reporters and photographers. We were told that he had a very high-pitched voice (like a woman talking) and that he was a tall person who walked straight. His entourage surrounded him, making him the centre of attraction.[23]

Leonard 'Charlie' May, a resident of Devizes all his life, also recalled the Americans. In 1943 he was working as a farm labourer. 'I worked pulling up mangels and got bored', so he applied for a job at Le Marchant Barracks with the American Transport Regiment and was accepted. Remembering those days, he recalled the generosity of the Americans in wartime Wiltshire:

It was the Americans who were paying me. I used to live by the hospital then and used to catch the bus from the Corn Exchange. I used to sign in at the guardroom, sign in with a Sergeant Goodall of the Wiltshire Regiment. The Americans were very generous. When Christmas came around, they used to give you a good meal and toys for the children. They even gave me a pair of waterproofs. The Yanks used to have some of their tanks parked along Quakers Walk, by the canal, all camouflaged up.[24]

Lil Painter also recalls the Americans in Devizes. From 1941 onwards she worked in Devizes station, checking goods on and off the train wagons:

They were a cheeky lot. If you were walking along the street with your husband, they used to come and join you, then pass remarks about you, your husband, anybody. They were always keen on ridiculous amounts of secrecy. I had never seen anything like it in my life. When they escorted the prisoners, which they sometimes did, there were always lots of high-ranking officers about.

We got to like them after a bit. You could always sell them a bottle of whisky to buy extra food and they were always kind in letting us have their rations. At one point, I was worked off my feet as the equipment for the hospitals came in by rail. We all used to help unload it. There was so much of it.[25]

By the beginning of August 1944, the 4th Armored Division was battling hard in Normandy as part of XX Corps. They were to end the war in Czechoslovakia nine hard months later. With the fighting units now in France, the Devizes camps were vacant once more. But not for long, however. The Allied planners had taken into consideration that they would require such camps to accommodate medical facilities for the wounded, as well as prisoner of war camps for the anticipated multitude of 'captured enemy personnel'. Devizes was now to receive its fair share of both.

Planning had got under way as early as the winter of 1943 for Waller and Prince Maurice Barracks to be occupied by the American 128th General Hospital and 141st General Hospital respectively. As in all military conversions, even to this day, civil manpower was required. Tenders thus went out from the Royal Engineers Works Services office at the Headquarters, Southern Command. By March 1944 all the necessary hard standings and additional roads had been completed, allowing for a second tender to go out for the conversion of the militia camps themselves. By mid-summer 1944, after the departure of the 37th Tank Battalion and 22nd Armored Field Artillery Regiment, the hospitals, their staff and equipment, were ready to move in. The 141st General Hospital was the first to be operational, in July, with the 128th General Hospital moving into Waller Barracks soon after and opening to receive casualties at 00.01 hours on 21 August 1944.[26]

The 128th General Hospital, like the 141st, was a large establishment. It was manned by 53 officers and doctors, 83 nurses and 452 enlisted men. Like the 4th Armored Division units before them, they too were not enamoured with the surroundings. The hospital's official War Diary had this to say:

The functions of the 128th (US) General Hospital are to treat patients requiring more than sixty days' hospitalisation as well as those requiring specialised treatment. Patients are received from station and other General Hospitals in the United Kingdom.

All personnel are quartered on the post in one-storey wood-frame buildings. Due to the large amount of supplies handled it was necessary to quarter some of the enlisted men in a gymnasium but the supplies were concentrated in three buildings and the enlisted men were able to occupy regular quarters. Bed space is regulated at 30 sq ft per man. Adequate toilets, showers or baths are not available due to the type of plumbing in each of the quarters.

The unit is operating three mess halls. One for the officers and nurses, one for the medical detachment and one for the patients. Considerable difficulty was encountered in becoming acquainted with the type of stove used for cooking but this has been overcome by usage. Adequate facilities are not available for washing dishes, pots and pans and utensils in the detachment mess and the officers' mess.[27]

The hospital was commanded by Colonel Leland E. Stilwell, a Reserve Officer recalled to the colours in 1941, having seen service in the First World War. He was the brother of the famous General 'Vinegar Joe' Stilwell who served in the Far East. In Devizes Colonel Stilwell was universally known as 'Mac'.

CHAPTER FOUR

Prisoners for Labour

Bleak eyes had this sullen band
arrogant in their shifting sideways stare,
eyes that had witnessed swift victory in other
lands – then reluctant surrender, chill despair . . .

William E. Morris ('The Captured')[1]

Enemy prisoners first came to Devizes in the autumn of 1941. These were Italians who had surrendered or been captured in North Africa during the Wavell offensives. Initially they were kept in camps in the desert in Egypt. In Britain at the same time, there was a distinct agricultural manpower shortage owing to many farmworkers having been called up. It was thus proposed that some of the large numbers of Italian prisoners be shipped to Britain to fill the shortfall. This was permissible under the Geneva Convention as such work could not be described as being war work.

On 9 September 1941 the Home Office issued a circular to all Chief Constables, informing them of the plan:

> I am directed by the Secretary of State to inform you that a scheme to bring to this country a number of Italian prisoners of war for employment as agricultural workers is now in operation . . .
>
> The scheme provides for the prisoners of war to be sent first to Transit Camps before being distributed to Labour Camps in the districts where they will be employed.
>
> It is estimated that approximately 6,000 prisoners of war will be accommodated in these camps by October; the scheme will then be held in abeyance until next spring when it is expected that a further 20,000 men will be established in other camps.[2]

The main driving force behind the scheme had been the County War Agricultural Executive Committees. These committees had been petitioning the Home Office and the Ministry of Agriculture for additional manpower for some time, largely because food production – crucial as the battle for the Atlantic was fought against the very successful German U-Boats – had started to fall.

Two transit camps were established, one at Prees Heath in Shropshire and the other at Lodge Moor in Sheffield. In turn, the labour camps for Southern Command were set up at Lambourn in Berkshire, Blackthorn near Oxford, and at Sudeley Castle in Gloucestershire. By the end of September 1941, some 1,480 Italian POWs were already working in the fields from these three camps, and this figure was to rise dramatically in 1942.

Many people can recall Italian prisoners working on the farms after 1942. Most of the prisoners were happy just to be out of the war, although a few others were not so. At first these prisoners were detailed off into large gangs to reduce the number of those needed to guard them. As the scheme grew and it became obvious that the Italians were not going to prove a security headache, groups of prisoners were assigned to individual farms throughout the country. By harvest time in 1943, some 7,000 were billeted in this way and the farmers themselves assumed the responsibility for the prisoners. In Devizes the first batch of twenty or so Italians were billeted in the Castle. Each day, transport would pick them up and distribute them to the various farms they were to be employed on. Later, in 1943, they moved to a small camp at Patney, close to Devizes, where they were to remain until repatriation in 1945.

The system worked very well, although sometimes the behaviour of the Italians caused consternation both to the local civilian population as well as the police. One of the primary concerns was caused by the often amorous inclinations shown by the prisoners. Work rates varied as well. John Perkins, the milkman and Home Guard member, recalls how the Italians 'would never work hard and refused to work at all if it was raining'.

Life changed dramatically for the Italians after Mussolini was ousted from power in September 1943 and the country joined the Allied cause. Italy was now an ally but it was not until 10 May 1944 that Italian POWs were recognised as such. In another letter to all Chief Constables, the Home Office further directed:

. . . to afford Italian prisoners of war in the United Kingdom an opportunity to cooperate in the common war effort by calling for volunteers who are prepared to undertake work directly connected with the operations of the war, in accordance with the declaration of co-belligerency made by the Italian Government.[3]

The plan envisaged asking Italian POWs if they would be prepared to cooperate with the Allies. Those who refused remained as prisoners under the same conditions as before. They were separated into 'Non-Cooperator Camps' and any breaking of the rules was to be met with 'rigorous and exemplary action'. Those who agreed to cooperate, however, would be allowed far greater freedoms. The camps they were in were no longer to be referred to as POW Camps, but as 'Italian Labour Battalions'. Also, the new 'former prisoners' would not have to wear the all-revealing POW uniforms with the letters 'PW' sewn onto them. Instead:

> Unpatched battle-dress dyed chocolate with FS cap of the same colour will be issued; shoulder titles with the word ITALY will be worn; camp police will wear a brassard; Italian badges of rank will be worn. Good conduct badges consisting of inverted chevrons may be worn on the left sleeve above the wrist.[4]

In August 1944 this uniform was changed to one of 'spruce green' with a service stripe of red, white and green below the title ITALY. The reason given for this change was that there would now be 'a contrast to the battle-dress worn by agricultural workers'.[5]

More importantly, the Italian volunteers were not to be referred to as prisoners of war but as 'cooperators' in all walks of life except official government correspondence with Rome or the International Red Cross in Switzerland. For the Italians, restrictions were also lifted on their individual freedom. All but the main fences of their camps would be removed and the gates left unlocked, even during the night. 'Cooperators' were permitted to go for walks or 'take other exercise' outside the camps during daylight hours up to a limit of some 2 miles from the main gate. Certain other freedoms, however, remained barred to them:

> The following restrictions will be retained on cooperators.
>
> (a) Whilst friendly relations with individuals whom they meet in the

course of their duty or in the place where they are billeted will not be forbidden, any relationship or attempt to establish relations with women of a sexual or amorous character will still be prohibited.

(b) Existing arrangements for censorship of correspondence will be maintained, and attempts to evade censorship are forbidden.[6]

By now, many Italians were actually billeted on the farms and other places of work to which they had been 'loaned out' by the Ministry of Agriculture. This made some of the rules of non-fraternisation simply untenable. Later, restrictions were relaxed and Italian cooperators were allowed to enter public or private premises as well as talk to people they came across! Those who remained in the labour camps were employed in groups of twelve or more, within a radius of 25 miles, usually working on menial tasks such as digging drainage ditches or on land reclamation projects. Italians were also used in the timber industry as well as in mining, quarrying, road repair and on the railways, unloading freight wagons.

★ ★ ★

While the Home Office and the Directorate of Prisoners of War discussed the colour of Italian uniforms, the war went on. On the morning of 6 June 1944, Allied troops stormed the Normandy beaches. This was to be the bloody, but final, struggle to defeat an enemy that attempted to rule the world with its New Order. Planning for the Second Front had first begun after the Casablanca Conference in January 1943. The man entrusted with the initial task was Lieutenant-General Sir Frederick Morgan. He was appointed as the Chief of Staff to the Supreme Allied Commander, General Eisenhower. Around him, General Morgan set up his committee, later known as the COSSAC Committee, or just COSSAC. One of the myriad minute details they had to plan for, was how to cope with the large number of prisoners expected to be captured once the Allies began to advance. The 21st Army Group alone, under the command of General Montgomery, had planned for the capture of around 500 prisoners a day initially, rising to 1,000 a day by D+10 (16 June).[7] This was perhaps too cautious as by D+3 (9 June) approximately 6,000 enemy personnel were already in their hands.[8]

Just inland from the British beach SWORD, near the French town of Colleville, nineteen-year-old Corporal Joseph Haeger was manning a post with others from the 4th Company of the 1st Battalion from Infantry Regiment 736, part of the 716th Infantry Division. In an interview nearly fifty years later, Joseph Haeger recounted his adventures to the author Russell Miller:

> I was a Catholic; my grandfather used to write to me regularly to say that he was praying for me and that God would protect me. I didn't believe in the war. My father told me back in 1939 that Germany could not possibly win and it would be like it was in the 1914–1918 war, when the whole world was against us.
>
> I was even more convinced that our position was hopeless when we arrived at Colleville. There were no defences worth talking about and although there was a great deal of work going on, planting obstacles and so forth on the beaches, everyone in the company knew that a good bombing would destroy everything.
>
> On the night of 5 June we sat around as usual talking about how badly prepared we were and when the invasion would come. At midnight, the bombing started. Although I felt the situation was hopeless, when the invasion actually started I knew that it was a battle for survival.[9]

Soon after, Joseph Haeger was indeed fighting for his life. He and those around him were ordered into a bunker, which was full of wounded men. Haeger again:

> There were about thirty of them lying on straw blankets, absolutely terrified and crying out all the time. There was hardly any air inside and a man in the observation hole shouted that the Canadians were starting to pile earth up against the ventilators. It started to get very hot and difficult to breathe. . . . The Battalion commander was firing a machine gun through a small aperture by the door. I will never forget the smell and the heat and noise inside the bunker, the cries of the wounded, the stink of exploding bullets and the gases from the machine gun. Just then the man in the observation post shouted: 'My God, they're bringing up a flame-thrower!'
>
> We heard the 'woof' of the flame-thrower, but the flames couldn't get through the staggered sections of the ventilation shaft, although it turned red-hot before our eyes. Now there was near panic . . .[10]

Haeger and his companions surrendered soon after, joining the slowly growing lines of ragged, dishevelled and exhausted prisoners being assembled on the beaches. Many were not German but Poles and Ukrainians, demonstrating the acute shortage of manpower the German Army was suffering after three years of bloody fighting against the Russians, their losses in North Africa and in Italy. But all these prisoners, German or otherwise, were to be transported across the Channel at the earliest opportunity, both for security reasons and to get them off the hands of the fighting troops.

Without doubt, Haeger would have suffered to some degree from 'shock of capture'. At the same time, his expressed religious nature and perceived failure of the war effort as a whole, would probably have meant that he would cooperate whole-heartedly with any interrogator.

Interestingly enough, the planning for dealing with the POWs in Normandy had altered very little from the 1940 plans. Captured enemy personnel were questioned for tactical information at battalion, brigade and divisional cages before being moved back to the beaches, where they were handed over to the Beach Groups. These 'groups' were composed of infantry battalions that were assigned the task of administering the beaches and ensuring the smooth operation of both in-loading men, stores and equipment and also of out-loading the wounded and prisoners of war, the latter usually crossing the Channel on empty tank landing ships. By this time, officers would have been separated from the NCOs and other ranks, prior to being entered into the POW administrative chain on landing in England.

The majority of Normandy prisoners came in through a number of ports all along the south coast including Southampton, Gosport and Weymouth. They were marched to nearby holding camps where they were divided up by name and rank. Further segregated into batches of fifty, they were marched once more to the railway station for onward movement to transit camps. These were often the older Command Cages or newly converted transit camps set up to cope with the ever increasing numbers.

Yet not every captured German came to Britain. As early as 1942, the British and American governments had agreed that each nation should be responsible for the prisoners its troops captured. The

Americans, however, did not initially agree to have the prisoners 'state-side'. For the Americans, the idea of having their prisoners on their native soil was novel and they had little experience in dealing with large numbers of POWs. The Joint Chiefs of Staff were also none too keen on the idea as they felt that Germany might retaliate against future American prisoners. At the same time, they argued, large numbers of German prisoners could constitute a threat against the American war industries that were just starting to gear themselves up. In the First World War, there had only been some 1,346 German prisoners housed, most of them being naval or merchant seamen. Indeed, even by November 1942, there were only some 431 prisoners of war on US soil – 380 Germans and 51 Japanese – and this at a time when 13,000 Germans captured after the battles in North Africa were entering the Canadian POW Camp at Lethbridge in Alberta.

The first test of this new cooperation came after the end of the Tunisian campaign in May 1943. The hundreds of thousands of Axis prisoners, it was agreed, would be transported to America. This would allow space in Britain for the influx of prisoners who would be captured once the campaign on the European mainland got under way. The responsibility for these prisoners would be divided equally. In May 1943 General Eisenhower is reported to have remarked to his staff in Tunisia:

> Why didn't some staff college ever tell us what to do with a quarter of a million prisoners so located at the end of a rickety railroad that it's impossible to move them and where guarding and feeding them is so difficult?[11]

The influx of German and Italian prisoners on to the American mainland soon got under way, however, and by December 1943 some 124,000 Germans and 50,000 Italians were settled in makeshift camps. So great was the flood that in 1943 the British Prime Minister himself had to share a passage across the Atlantic on the *Queen Mary* with 5,000 Germans. Churchill wrote:

> About five thousand German prisoners were already on board. It had been suggested that they should be transferred to another ship, but I

could not see what harm they could do to us, under due control and without weapons, and, since the point was referred to me, had given instructions that they should come along.[12]

By the end of the war in Europe, there were some 155 main camps with a further 511 satellite compounds spread through forty-four of the forty-eight American states. It was also estimated that some $50 million was spent on building new camps and refurbishing older ones. The Geneva Convention was adhered to very strictly, with each enlisted man having 40 sq. ft of space, and each officer some 120 sq. ft. But if prisoners had to live under canvas for a time, so did their guards.[13]

The first group of German prisoners captured on D-Day, 364 in all, crossed the Channel from Normandy on 7 June 1944. They landed in the evening at Southampton where they were segregated, fed and bedded down for the night. The following morning, they were entrained once more, arriving at Kempton Park racecourse for screening. Kempton had by now been renamed No. 9 Reception Camp and it was here that Alexander Scotland had established one of his PWIS(H) screening teams. From Kempton Park, those prisoners selected for deeper, longer term interrogations were moved to CSDIC, by now in Beaconsfield, or to the London Cage. The rest were moved to Command Transit Camps for detailed documentation, administration, medical checks and delousing. Normally they would spend only a day or two there, before moving once again to their final POW Camp. By this stage each prisoner had been categorised 'White', 'Grey' or 'Black', depending on his perceived political outlook. To begin with, this was a very hit-and-miss system as often the grading could be affected by the slightest incident. Many prisoners, especially the SS, parachute troops and U-Boat crews, were fully imbued with the National Socialist ethos, which had been drilled into them throughout their military service. To many Germans, therefore, not to be graded 'Black' would have been seen as a failure among their fellow inmates.

Gunther Schran, who served as an anti-aircraft gunner in northern France for most of the war, was taken into captivity when the men from his battery forced their commanding officer to surrender to the Canadians on 23 September 1944, the day after Boulogne fell to the

Canadian 3rd Infantry Division. Schran 'failed' his political classification screening at Kempton Park. In an interview he made for the Imperial War Museum Sound Archive, he recalled:

> At Kempton Park I was interviewed first of all and asked questions such as 'Can Germany still win the war?' Of course, being a cocky so-and-so, I said 'Yes, of course they will – you'll see', more out of spite than out of conviction, I'm sure. Of course, that probably made me, straight away, somebody who had to be sent away under heavy guard.
>
> You see, they had this classification: 'A's were the anti-Nazis, 'B's were the middle of the road and 'C's, apparently, were the Nazis. And of course it was something against the Geneva Convention – you are not allowed to classify a prisoner in any political way whatsoever. So again, out of spite, we protested against this, which, of course, probably meant that we were all classified 'C'.[14]

Schran was sent to Comrie Camp in Scotland, one of the harder camps, about which we shall hear more later.

Miriam Kochan in her book *Prisoners of England* interviewed a former German prisoner, Siegfried Gabler, who was captured by the Americans around St Lo in August 1944. After working in Cherbourg unloading stores for several weeks, he was eventually transported across the Channel. Gabler recalled:

> Then they put us into a boat. We thought we were going to America. We spent two days and two nights in the boat. It was one of those landing craft with no doors and no windows so we couldn't see where we were going. Then we landed. The first thing we saw were some old gas lamps, and we said 'This isn't America!' It was Portland Bill. The date was October 1944.
>
> Everybody had to go through Kempton Park. There, they stripped your bodies as well as your brains. They investigated who you were, where you came from. They asked questions like 'When did you last see your father?' Then we were all split up. I was sent to Glen Mill Camp, Oldham (Camp 176).[15]

There is no evidence in surviving records to suggest that prisoner questioning was ever undertaken using violent, physical means. Certainly Scotland stresses this in his own writings. However, with many refugees and other European nationals involved in the process, it is very possible that physical as well as verbal abuses did occur.

Another former prisoner interviewed by Miriam Kochan, Siegfried Bandelow, had this to say:

> On 30 August 1944 I was taken prisoner by the Americans, together with the rest of my Corps. I was a lieutenant in charge of [a] company . . . I had been wounded in the leg and arm. On 16 September I was in a military hospital at St Mere-Eglise. Then it was Cherbourg and we crossed the Channel to arrive in Southampton on 21 October. From there I was taken to Hampden Park and London. We were very badly treated by the military police and some pretty aggressive guards. I was sent for interrogation at the London District Cage, where I was asked questions about things and situations I knew nothing about. The last private possessions which the Americans had left me (photos and letters) were taken away and my spectacles and stick were broken beyond repair. To this day, I do not know the reason for all this, as I was a member of an ordinary rifle unit and never a member of the Party.[16]

The guards' behaviour is perhaps understandable, though not excusable, as at this time V2s were falling thick and fast on to London and the south-east counties.

CHAPTER FIVE

New Camps for Old

To be a prisoner has always seemed
to me about the worst thing that
could happen to a man.

John Buchan (*Greenmantle*, 1916)[1]

It is difficult to give the precise date when the first German prisoners actually arrived in Devizes. Obviously the odd *Luftwaffe* crewman had passed through prior to 1944. The earliest written record found by the author was on a photograph held in the National Archives in America. It is captioned 'Tec-4 George G. Whitney . . . helps newly arrived prisoners to file their processing forms. This is the first step in processing. 16 July 1944.' These first prisoners were probably held in Le Marchant Camp on the London Road, the first of many thousands who were to be found there until the middle of 1946. Le Marchant Camp had been selected towards the end of 1943 by Headquarters, Southern Command, as a potential POW camp. By then, alongside the wooden huts, thirty Romney huts had been erected. These were larger versions of the ubiquitous Nissen huts and could each house upwards of 700 prisoners, sleeping on three-tier bunk beds. Six of these huts still remain, now housing the vehicles, machinery and stores of Wiltshire County Council's Highways Department.

In British records, Le Marchant Camp is first mentioned in the papers of the Prisoner of War Directorate, Department 1a (PW-1(A)). On 7 September 1944 their equivalent of a War Diary records:

Memo to Southern Command that Le Marchant Camp Devizes is to operate as No. 23 PW Camp for German prisoners of war as from 11 Sept 44. Personnel attached for administration purposes to No. 144 Italian Labour Battalion.[2]

One of the first administrative staff to arrive was Captain Richard Hurn, a member of the Royal Artillery. He had served in North Africa and had then been on the staff of the 8th Army Headquarters in Italy where he had had the task of reconnoitring for suitable locations for the Headquarters as it followed the ebb and flow of battle up through Italy. When Mrs Hurn required a serious operation in the late summer of 1944, he was granted compassionate leave to be with her. While in England, the personnel branch of the Royal Artillery at Woolwich suggested that he might be interested in a local posting as the Adjutant of Le Marchant POW Camp, which he readily accepted. Over fifty years later, Dick Hurn has a keen memory of his time at the camp:

> My wife was due an operation and I was given a compassionate posting with six weeks' leave. When I visited Woolwich I was asked if I knew anything about prisoners of war. When I arrived, the camp was empty although opposite there were a lot of Americans in the hospitals.
>
> The Commanding Officer was a very good former cavalry officer called John Trelawny Upton. He had commanded a camp before and brought with him a German messing officer called Goertz and a German interpreter called Reis who was a refugee from before the war. The chief interpreter was another 'Gunner' called Captain Craig. . . . You must realise that the chief interpreter was a very important man as he was also the senior intelligence officer for the camp. Other staff included a large Quartermaster's department which was run by 'old sweats' and therefore run extremely well.[3]

Captain Hurn and his team did not have long to set up their camp for its first role as a transit camp. Meanwhile, over the Channel in France the capture of Caen and the American break-out had ended the stalemate. In August, the Falaise Gap was closed. As the Allied air forces decimated the German columns caught within, Axis soldiers of every description, colour and creed surrendered. Many, as mentioned before, were not even German. Many of those living in Devizes clearly remember Mongolian-looking prisoners as they were marched from the railway station to the camp, heads bowed and wearing the remains of distinctive lightish-green uniforms.

The system devised by the camp staff for administering the prisoners as they arrived and then departed the next day had to be efficient and streamlined. Captain Hurn recalls:

The first POWs arrived after the Falaise battles and we started to get very busy. We would be contacted by the RTO [Railway Transportation Officer] at Southampton who would give us the number of trains due to move to Devizes and their time of arrival. Each train would have 500 prisoners on board. These trains usually arrived in the late afternoon or early evening and they would be met by members of the Military Police company attached to us. The prisoners would then be marched from the station to the camp where we had a system to process them.

On the square we had a series of tables in front of some of the huts. The prisoners would be searched for any documents and then stripped of any uniform. This included any leather items, such as belts and pouches, as well as their issue knives, forks, spoons and mugs they always seemed to carry. From there, they were given a thorough medical examination. We had five or six German doctors and they would check them all over. As you can imagine, many had scabies or were lousy and they had to be sprayed with delousing powder which got everywhere. Next, they went to the shower blocks prior to being fed in the cook houses and then issued bedding for the night.

Next morning, we would give them breakfast and issue further rations to cover their journey to their permanent camp. On average, we would administer 2,500 prisoners in and out each day.

The escorting military policemen were not the usual Red Caps but Blue Caps. These men had been initially recruited back in the dark days of the invasion threat, when they had been used to guard key points throughout the country. Now they were being put to use as prisoner escorts. Their job was to ensure that all prisoners reached their destinations. There were upwards of a thousand such military policemen based in Le Marchant Camp for such tasks although they were rarely seen in town. They were often away for up to three days at a time, escorting prisoners all over the country.

By 1 September the First British Corps had crossed the River Seine and were thrusting westward towards Le Havre while the Guards Armoured Division of XXX Corps reached Arras. One of the German units encountered in the area around Amiens was the remnants of the 203rd Artillery Regiment, a motorised artillery battalion. Klaus Steffen was with the unit that day, fighting hard. Brought up in Silesia of Catholic stock, Steffen had never joined the Hitler Youth nor the Nazi Party. This had been noted by the authorities who refused him a place at university because of it. Called up in October 1940, he joined 3 Artillery Regiment of 3 Infantry Division and found himself in northern France in early 1941 where his duties included liaison with the local civilians. That summer, the division was moved east and involved from the outset during the attack on Russia, where it was eventually decimated during the siege of Stalingrad.

Klaus Steffen was luckier than most. He contracted jaundice and was hospitalised, and ended up back in France to recuperate. As manpower became short, the Germans started to form 'stomach' battalions, comprised of men who were more sick than fit to fight. Steffen was part of this call-up, and he joined the 203rd. Captured on 1 September, he later recalled the friendly treatment he received from the tank crews who first handled him. Quickly passed back down the POW chain, the standard of treatment steadily began to fall as first he was delivered to a cage run by French-Canadian troops and then the French Army of the Interior – The 'Marquis' – who administered a holding cage near the Pas de Calais.

Steffen crossed the Channel on 16 September and docked at Southampton. He was one of the many who passed through Le Marchant Camp several days later, before moving on to a camp near Oldham. He was not so enamoured with his time at Devizes:

> [In Southampton] we were put into cages which must have been quickly erected. We were given a blanket and told we would sleep there for the night, which we did.
>
> The next morning we were put on a train and ended up in Devizes, in Wiltshire. We were marched to a huge complex. I can still see it. I don't know whether it [was] an Army thing or a university thing, or school, but it was a huge area with big buildings on one side. There we were separated into Army, Air Force, Navy – whatever – and they were most keen to find people belonging to the SS.
>
> My lasting impression of my three-day stay there was the abuse that was hurled at us by people in British uniforms, but obviously not Englishmen; foreigners, Poles perhaps or Czechs, I don't know. We were not physically ill-treated but definitely verbally. The abuse was absolutely disgusting – you know, they addressed us as 'swine' all the time for a start. It really was demoralising. That's something that, after my earlier experiences of someone in British uniform, rather changed things.[4]

Steffen's experiences at Devizes are startling although perhaps not too surprising. He was among the first prisoners to arrive at the camp and there were indeed many foreign nationals in the Pioneer Corps companies used as guard troops. His mention of the word 'swine' should also be noted: it was to feature many times in December 1944, used by some Germans about others. But the experience cannot have been too distressing for Klaus Steffen. He qualified as a camp interpreter and remained in the Yorkshire area throughout 1946, before volunteering to join the re-education programmes at Beaconsfield. While a prisoner he met and married a local girl and has remained in this country ever since.

'Charlie' May was one of those who used to help out when the prisoners arrived at Le Marchant Camp. He recalled that 'they used to be lined up on the square where we would take their uniforms and cut the buttons off. We would then put them in bags for the Army to take away and burn'. The bits of uniform that were retained were stored in a small depot opposite the camp. It is said that many locals could be seen wearing a German Army belt once this 'treasure trove' had been discovered by local schoolboys!

The sight, sound and smell of those columns of German prisoners as they made their way to and from the railway station can never be forgotten by the town's residents. The arrival of some of the first prisoners was recorded in the diary of a young railway enthusiast, William Crosbie-Hill. A week after the D-Day landings he wrote:

The human cargo discharged are German POWs, among the very first taken capture following the Normandy invasion the week before. Brought by transport ship to Weymouth, they have entrained . . . for the journey to a cleansing station at Devizes Camp. They will be sent in a couple of days later to a POW camp somewhere in Scotland. Dirty and unshaven and predominantly grey-looking, many walk surrender-fashion with both arms raised aloft. A few officers with ankle-length greatcoats carry themselves with a straight-faced determination, perhaps due more to a knowledge of the Geneva Convention than out of a greater degree of personal courage. The whole procession marched off, the pathetic and the proud, with their armed guard for the two-mile walk to Roundway camp.

The policemen who had attended to keep back the attention of the civil populace also leave but apart from a young porter, Mr Bond the foreman and a friend . . . I am the only onlooker at this surprisingly unexpected event.[5]

Joy Pride, née Matthews, also remembers those first prisoners arriving in Devizes. Evacuated from London because of the Blitz, Joy was living in Devizes with her uncle, Jim Gaiger, and his family. Jim was the camp's Clerk of Works. His duties were to ensure that the building structures, wire fences, guard towers and the like, were in tip-top condition. If anything structural fell apart, he fixed it. Fifty-one years later, Joy vividly recalls:

Living with my aunts and uncle – Jim Gaiger – at Rotherstone, Devizes, we knew, perhaps before others, that German POWs were coming to [the] Devizes camps.

I remember going down to the station, now long gone, to see the first POW trains come in. I don't know what I expected, but not the loads of scruffy, dirty, grey-uniformed men with an odd smell about them that piled out and were lined up on the platforms, guarded by soldiers with guns and bayonets fixed.

I know how much I thought I hated them, as like many others we had lost family and friends. I didn't stay and ran home, only to find out that the POWs were marched through Rotherstone anyway on their way to the camps. First came some motorcycle outriders, I suppose to ensure clear roads, then long columns of POWs guarded by either British or American soldiers. They [the prisoners] looked tired and beaten and some looked relieved to be out of it all.

At the end of the columns came the Nazi officers; they were entirely different – cold, hard and arrogant – some marching, some even goose-stepping and I know we 'booed' them.

Towards the end of the arrivals the columns were made up of mostly old men and young lads, anyone it seemed, who could carry a gun.

One Nazi officer, we were told afterwards, had demanded transport at the station, then refused to walk. He landed up at the end of the column only in his socks, being encouraged along by a huge black GI with his fixed bayonet (I admit we cheered).[6]

Mrs Hehir, the ATS girl who had worked in the Le Marchant Barracks Quartermaster's department, also remembers the prisoners arriving. She recalled:

The first prisoners of war arrived after D-Day. They used to march them up from the station to the camp and no one knew when they were coming. The police used to escort them, out front, moving bicycles and the like, out of the way. One or two wouldn't march so they were pushed along.[7]

John Perkins, the anti-tank gunner in the Devizes Home Guard used to man a post at the station:

> I used to guard the Devizes railway station which also had a petrol store. At first we had a lot of trouble bringing up the prisoners. They had planned to build a separate railway siding by the Fox & Hounds [to the east of the town] but never did. US troops were the first to escort the prisoners. They always had a lot of men armed with machine guns. After a bit, anyone did it, sometimes even wounded British soldiers going home on leave.[8]

Schoolboy David Knapman lived in a house beside the railway line just along from Devizes station. He often saw the train carriages full of prisoners as they set off for the permanent camps:

> At the bottom of the garden, which sloped downhill, was an orchard and then a retaining wall. There was then a drop of 6 ft on to the railway line. Usually we could only see the tops of the railway carriages from the house, beyond which were open fields.
>
> For some reason, which I have never found out, they used to let the train free-wheel out of the station down the hill, where it would wait for up to five minutes, opposite our back garden. The prisoners used to ask us for apples off the trees. Sometimes we felt sorry for them and just lobbed them across. Other times we would throw them very hard! It always amazes me to this day, how many of them could speak English.[9]

★ ★ ★

In the same way that the Italian prisoners were used on the fields and in the forests, so too were the Germans. Use of this source of manpower, however, was not as easy. Due to the screening of the political views of the prisoners, many were classed as not employable. None the less, on 23 August 1944 the Home Office wrote to all Chief Constables:

> It has been decided that selected German prisoners of war shall be employed in the United Kingdom on agriculture and forestry, up to 16,000 being selected for this purpose in the first instance. They are to work in gangs of 12 or more (but not exceeding 25) with armed escort, and are to be accommodated in existing Italian camps, the Italians being housed in other vacant accommodation in the same areas as far as possible.

In addition the War Office have agreed to the employment, principally on salvage work, of German prisoners of war by the American Army. Arrangements have been made for Chief Officers of Police to be informed of the local employment of German prisoners in this way through the Police Liaison Officers with the United States Forces.[10]

Initially, of course, this decision did not affect Le Marchant Camp which continued in its role as a transit camp. As autumn gave way to winter, however, the volume of prisoners started to fall as the *Wehrmacht* withdrew behind the Rhine to consolidate and regroup. The Devizes camp began to retain small numbers of prisoners until, by about October 1944, there was a permanent camp cadre. The majority of these were classified as 'Whites' or 'Greys' and thus could go out to work under the POW Employment Scheme.

In November 1944 it was decided to make POW Camp 23 a permanent camp to allow work gangs to be based there. Unfortunately, the numbers envisaged for the camp were greater than the available hutted accommodation decreed by the Geneva Convention. The War Diary of Headquarters Salisbury Plain and Dorset District (SPDD) recorded that November:

At 23 PW camp Devizes, additional facilities were put in hand to meet the new commitment for this camp – i.e. 7,500 German p/ws in permanent residence. It was expected this could be accepted by 30 Nov 44, as follows:

In covered accommodation	6,170
In tents	1,330
Total	7,500[11]

A month later, the same Headquarters was to record:

The District Command authorised the provision of 46 Nissen Huts at 23 PW Camp to replace single tentage at present in use. These are being removed from abandoned S/L [searchlight] sites and re-erected by German PW labour, and will provide covered accommodation for the total complement of the camp. Official WO [War Office] approval is still awaited but work is well advanced.[12]

That same month, some of the German workers were already employed, keeping the roads clear of mud. The War Diary again:

Three working parties, each of 50 German PWs from Camp 23, have been organised by this HQ under escort to work on public and military roads. This expedient has proved helpful in preventing the large deposits of mud brought on to the roads by tracked vehicles, which at times caused cancellation of civil bus services.[13]

Although the German work gangs laboured hard to keep the roads clear, Hitler's Ardennes Offensive did a far better job. Caught unawares, all available Allied forces were rushed to the area to stem any breakthrough. Those American units still in the UK, most of them only recently landed and still training, left their camps in a hurry. Headquarters SPDD, in turn, found more work for the Devizes prisoners. The War Diary for January 1945 noted:

At PW camp 23, sufficient accommodation to house all PWs under cover was completed by the first week in Jan. To the three German working parties already operating, was added a further party of 200, who were set to work on road maintenance in Tidworth under escorts supplied by Southern Comd. Tidworth roads have suffered from prolonged occupation of the barracks by US Armored formations. On the whole, in spite of snow, very few road problems have been encountered in this normally difficult month, thanks to the absence of armour.[14]

Although not imprisoned in Devizes until May 1945, Emil Flemming was one of those who soon found himself out and about on the farms. Born and brought up in Pomerania, then in eastern Germany but now in Poland, Emil had been stationed on Alderney as an anti-aircraft gunner. On the restoration of British sovereignty to the Islands in May 1945, Emil Flemming was shipped to Southampton and then on to Devizes:

I arrived in Devizes on 18 May 1945, very undernourished. In fact I only weighed 125 lb because we had no rations in the Channel Islands. By harvest time I was out in the fields and I stayed on to to help a cowman until February 1946. By this stage, there were about 100 German prisoners in the Italian camp at Patney, also working.

I was also part of a group that went to Ogbourne St George, peeling potatoes in a US transit camp there. Some of us peeled while others worked delousing American soldiers before they went home! The Yanks could never understand why we wore our greatcoats in the summer. We were stealing salamis out of the cook-house.[15]

Some work gangs worked from the camp itself, being collected each morning by their employers. Locals sent to collect them recall that the prisoners would be paraded on the camp square opposite a series of numbered boards. Each task was allotted a number and the prisoners behind that number would be the labour for that day.

In Devizes there was also a small number of non-working 'Blacks' and, as in many camps throughout the country, these prisoners started to take over the daily running of the compounds within the confines of the wire. Consequently, discipline in the German camps often existed on two levels: that imposed from outside by the camp staff and guards; and that on the inside imposed by the prisoners themselves.

Richard Garrett, who wrote *P.O.W.* in 1981, investigated this, quoting the German prisoner Fritz Wentzel:

> We all had to live together, and so each of us had the right to expect a certain degree of order and consideration from the others. If we could all do just as we liked, life would become intolerable. In a POW camp, the need for order is so great, that it even justifies a certain degree of compulsion. By that, I don't mean spineless submission.[16]

Some camps earned themselves a reputation, both inside and out, depending on the categories of prisoners held within. Several camps were known to be hard, especially No. 18 Camp at Featherstone Park and No. 21 at Comrie in Perthshire, while others were less so. The British authorities took some time to recognise the fact that certain camps had too many 'Blacks' imprisoned together, who were thus able to continue to pursue the Nazi cause from within. This led to all sorts of trouble, including escape attempts and murder, that could have been avoided. Much, of course, was down to the individual British camp commandants and their staff and guards. The commandants were chosen with some care, although the odd 'loose cannon' slipped through the selection net. Most commandants, however, proved to be ideal for the job, especially after the failure of the Ardennes Offensive in January 1945, and the final surrender in May when prisoner morale slipped to rock-bottom.

Those detailed to act as guard forces at each camp were usually men from the Pioneer Corps, graded unfit for active service or deemed so after being wounded. All orders tried to ensure that prisoners were treated firmly but fairly, although sometimes this was difficult. Some of the Pioneer Corps companies were later replaced by Polish troops, a decision that, in hindsight, was unwise. By the war's end, there were ten Polish Guard Companies (PGC), and there was no love lost between them and their charges. No. 5 PGC served in Devizes, and No. 7 PGC in Comrie.

The German camps in the UK were usually divided up into compounds, primarily for ease of administration. Sometimes each compound held prisoners from the same arm of service, as was the case in Devizes. Other camps, especially often after the war was over, tended to house prisoners according to their political category. Within each compound there was usually a small self-administering staff chosen by the prisoners themselves to represent the compound to the higher authorities. Usually this staff would report to the prisoner camp leader, or 'Lagerführer' who, in turn, would report to the British camp commandant. Selection of the prisoners' camp leader was normally voted on by the prisoners' compound staff, but in some cases he was selected by the British authorities.

All camps had a similar routine which was largely centred around roll-call, meal times, lock-up and lights out. Walter Herkstroeter, a U-Boat radar technician, was imprisoned in Devizes after the end of the war. His U-Boat – U-1277, a deep-sea 'schnorkel' boat – was scuttled off the Portuguese coast in May 1945, with Walter eventually reaching the UK in June. The routine he recalls in Devizes was probably little changed since 1944:

Breakfast was at 8 a.m., lunch between 12 a.m. and 1 p.m. with the evening meal between 5 and 6 p.m. The food was not too good either.[17]

Food played a big part of any prisoner's life. Meal times not only relieved the boredom, if only for short periods during the day, but they also gave the prisoners the opportunity to collect foodstuffs that could be used to barter with at a later date. The camp authorities, of course, watched this very carefully to prevent food being stored for possible escape attempts. It must not be forgotten, however, that there was severe rationing in Britain at the time. Under the Geneva Convention, prisoners of war must be fed the same standard of food with the same calorific value as home-based garrison troops.

Consequently, prisoners tended to be better off than those outside the wire. According to Richard Garrett, each prisoner should have received some 3,300 calories a day. Because of worldwide shortages, this had been dropped to 2,800 for working prisoners and as low as 2,000 calories for those who remained behind the wire. Garrett went on to quote a study by Professor Mitscherlich who was researching the standard of calorie intake among returning German prisoners. Some 67 per cent of prisoners stated that the food was poor to start with but had steadily improved; 48 per cent declared that they had been continually hungry at the beginning of their captivity; and a high 76 per cent confirmed that by the end of their imprisonment, they were never hungry.[18] It would be interesting to compare the last figure against the percentages of working to non-working prisoners. Certainly those who were billeted on the farms were much better off. Several former prisoners interviewed by the author remember being able to have as much bread, milk, butter, cheese and eggs as they wanted. One prisoner even recalls being able to have a pound of local cheese at a time. The national ration was two ounces a week!

While many German prisoners had the opportunity to work outside their camps, thus to some extent relieving the boredom of imprisonment, the rest languished behind the wire. To ease the tedium, many prisoners turned to skills they had acquired in civilian life. Each camp usually had its fair share of musicians, choirs and sports teams. Classes were often established, teaching many different subjects. Both the British authorities and the International Red Cross based in Switzerland supported such initiatives. In Devizes the prisoners soon became well known for their manufacture of wooden toys, slippers made from sacking and cardboard, as well as any number of metal items such as cigarette cases and lighters. These they often used for barter, primarily for cigarettes, money not being permitted inside the camps.

John Perkins remembers some of the items the prisoners in Devizes made:

They used to make all sorts of things to swap for cigarettes. Shoes, brushes, even miniature boats in bottles. Presumably these were made by the Navy prisoners.[19]

Walter Herkstroeter recalled:

> In the camp, we had every trade available. Since we only got paid five shillings and sixpence a week in 'camp money' – we weren't allowed to have English money – we did everything we could. We made slippers out of sacking and such like. I remember they were very strict on us having tins.[20]

Emil Flemming recalled the slipper trade very readily:

> Our biggest problem was boredom. Those going to work on the farms were told to keep their eyes open, and not just for things we could use ourselves. On the farms we used to collect all the sacking cloth we could, while those in the towns collected cardboard. We used then to sell our cigarettes giving us money to buy dye. Those remaining in the camp each day used to dye the sacks, pull them apart strand by strand, and then plait the strands to make slippers with cardboard soles. These we used to make to order for the local civilians. At Christmas time in 1945, the manager of a Devizes shoe shop complained. He couldn't sell any slippers at all![21]

As autumn turned to winter, Devizes and many other German and Italian camps throughout the UK settled down to what many hoped would be the last winter of the war. To some, however, hope of a different kind – of the final, true victory – had been rekindled. V2 rockets, one of Hitler's 'wonder-weapons', were now falling in and around London as the V1s had done before them. Even the Belgian port of Antwerp, the new Allied main supply port across the Channel, was under fire from these silent rockets. Their new hope led to events that winter in Devizes which would shock many and have far-reaching consequences.

CHAPTER SIX

An Honourable Pastime

Stone walls do not a prison make,
Nor iron bars a cage.

Richard Lovelace[1]

Escape from captivity during wartime has often been viewed by the British as an 'honourable pastime'. More than ever, during the Second World War, officers and men were expected to attempt to escape given the right opportunity, conditions and organisation. The escaping philosophy was first brought home to the public by Winston Churchill. Escaping from Boer captivity to freedom in Mozambique in 1899, his adventures captivated the mood of the time. The international press built up the story to such a degree that the set-backs in South Africa, and there were many, were put to one side by the press and the general public. Churchill's escape took on an air of romantic 'derring-do', a national frame of mind that persisted throughout the First World War. Interestingly enough, there were more German and Austrian attempted escapes in the First World War than Allied. Perhaps it was the sheer distances that daunted Allied escapees, needing to cross Europe to reach friendly lines, while the Germans had to travel only a relatively short distance to a port and passage home if they could successfully stow away on board a ship or steal a boat. None of the attempts were successful, always being frustrated by the fact that Britain is an island. That final effort to find passage across the Channel or the North Sea, or even across the Irish Sea into internment, has always seemed to defeat escapees.

With the drawing-up of the Geneva Convention after the First World War, escape was recognised as a de facto attitude of mind, almost a recognised action in wartime. Prisoners, the Convention stated, could not be tried by the detaining power for the act of escaping. However, if during the escape attempt, a civilian or military crime was committed – an assault on a guard, theft of clothing and so on – then the detaining power did have the right to try the escapee in the normal civilian or military courts. During the Second World War, all sides respected the idea of escape as an honourable one, but those caught were treated very differently. At one end of the spectrum were the Japanese, who showed no mercy. They recognised the honour in attempting to escape, and indeed expected it, but still executed those who were subsequently caught. The Germans, together with their cooperating partners, such as the Vichy French and pro-Fascist Italian elements, expected prisoners to try to escape, but took a tough line against any who were caught. This culminated in the shooting of fifty Allied escapees from Stalag Luft III at Sagan in March 1944. Unfortunately, those caught were dressed in civilian clothing and were therefore handled by the civilian authorities. Coupled to this, the Nazi prospects with regards to the war – they were not doing well on the eastern fronts and an invasion was looming in the west – led to ever harsher orders and instructions as regarded the Home Front. Consequently, the Sagan escapees were murdered individually where they were picked up. This pathetic finale revealed in 1944, perhaps for the first time to many in the civilised world, the depths to which the Nazi regime was rapidly sinking.

In Britain and the Empire countries, Axis prisoners were initially regarded in a very 'matter-of-fact' manner. The Geneva Convention pervaded all thought with regard to captured personnel and quite rightly so. All records available today point to a genuine desire to be correct – firm but fair – but at the same time they demonstrate a naiveté of initial thought. German personnel captured at the beginning of the war, mostly naval, U-Boat and *Luftwaffe* aircrew, tended to be regarded in a 'what-ho Jerry!' fashion. There were individuals like Scotland at PWIS(H) and others at CSDIC and MI19 who could appreciate the serious need to build up and maintain a system whereby the whole of the POW chain was handled by professional people with professional attitudes. There could be no room for camp commandants who would universally be seen as the archetypal 'Colonel Blimps'. By the beginning of 1944, each camp commandant was carefully selected, those chosen often having had former POW experiences in the First World War. Then perhaps, lethargy set in. Within months of the Allied landings in Normandy, it became obvious that the war would end in Allied victory. The German Army was faltering. The standard of the majority of German soldiers verged on the pathetic. The younger, teenage recruits, the sick of the 'stomach' battalions, the 'Volksturm', Germany's home guard, all pointed to a military force that was facing collapse. The only question, really, was when? The general feeling of the British population who watched the sad lines of captured enemy personnel shuffle their way into captivity was one of growing sympathy. This did not extend to the often arrogant officers or SS prisoners, but included the ordinary soldiers, called up to fight in a war they did not really want or understand. A rather surprising letter was circulated to all Chief Constables by the then Director General of MI5, Sir David Petrie, who wrote to Sir Alexander Maxwell at the Home Office on 19 October 1944. In his letter, the views Petrie expressed about the general security situation in the country at the time are difficult to understand, even with hindsight. He wrote:

> Although the war is not yet ended, one can but look upon the 'stand down' order to the Home Guard and the easing of black-out restrictions as a tacit acknowledgement that the last serious risk to internal security has been removed. The brunt of this struggle, now successfully ended, has fallen on the Police and the Security Service, each with their separate responsibilities but partners in the main one.[2]

Less than two months later, the situation was very different, the war far from ended.

In total, it is thought that by March 1945 there had been more than 400 Axis escape attempts from camps all over the world. At that time, only four prisoners continued to evade capture. The majority of escape attempts failed for a variety of reasons, the primary one being bad planning. Escape, just as any other military operation, requires detailed organisation. A prisoner cannot just leave his camp and expect to walk or ride home. In wartime he has to pass as a local or friendly Allied national. He has to have documentation, an alibi and so on. More importantly, he must have the desire to succeed. Many writers in the past forty years or so have commented on the perception that perhaps the German POWs of 1939–45 did not have the right mental attitude for escape. Permanently regimented back home, the idea of individualism so necessary for a successful escape was literally alien to them. There were, of course, some notable exceptions. Franz von Werra, the *Luftwaffe* fighter pilot shot down in September 1940, made several escape attempts while in Britain. He eventually succeeded in Canada in 1941, walking into America which was then still neutral to a degree, having jumped from a train taking him to his new camp. Three German Afrika Korps soldiers escaped from an Indian camp, making their way to the Japanese lines in Burma during 1943. Then there were the Italians in Kenya who escaped to climb Mount Kenya and then returned themselves to captivity. All of these escapes were exceptions to the general rule.

The Allied attitude to German and Italian escape attempts was expressed by Dick Hurn, the Adjutant at Devizes. He said:

> You were bound to get escape attempts . . . people were being found outside the wire all the time. One day, I remember, I was called by the Police and had to pick up two Germans who had been found near Upavon airfield. Another time, we had a prisoner who made it to Dover. He was found in a motor boat trying to start it. He had even bought some petrol for it from a British Army lorry driver.[3]

The standard punishment for escape attempts was up to twenty-eight days in solitary confinement, sometimes on a punishment diet of bread and water, and strictly supervised to ensure no breach of conventions. Such penalties would hardly deter a serious would-be escapee, and consequently many did attempt to escape, if only to relieve the boredom.

Another factor that must have adversely affected the chances of successful escapes by German prisoners was that they had had no schooling in either evasion before capture or escape after capture. The ordinary German soldier was not expected to be captured. Rather like the Russians, the German soldier was expected to die fighting to the last bullet, not to surrender. This attitude enhanced the 'shock of capture' when they were caught, and at the same time, almost certainly produced the feeling among the still faithful Nazis that they had betrayed the National Socialist cause. But having failed the cause once by being captured in the first place, they might make amends inside the camps by ensuring that they demonstrated their true allegiance, which they also forced upon others. More importantly, under the Geneva Convention, they were permitted to do so. For instance, the Nazi salute was not banned in British camps until May 1945.

★ ★ ★

Once Camp 23 at Devizes had been fully integrated into the role of a permanent camp, life settled down somewhat. Gone were the hectic days of the transit camp and the daily rotations of some 2,500 prisoners. For the permanent staff, the administration of some 7,500 permanent prisoners was a task in itself. The first few days in November 1944 were quite busy as the Canadians and Royal Marine Commandos stormed the island of Walcheren in the Scheldt Estuary. Victory, everyone hoped, was not far away. The Home Guard was on the verge of being stood down and even the stringent black-out rules were relaxed to what became known as the 'dim-out', where full black-out conditions were only applied during alerts. V2s were still falling but little could be done about that until the firing lines in Europe had been overrun. In Camp 23 and others around the country, the morale of the POW community was not good. Germany was losing the war, a fact that could only be whispered among the prisoners for fear of being overheard by the 'Rollkommandos' who continued to guard the National Socialist ideals even behind the wire. For, under the very eyes of the Allied guards and camp staffs, ad hoc groups of prisoners had formed themselves into self-appointed guardians of the Nazi cause, believing fervently in the 'final victory' they had been promised by a Führer who now, more than ever, maintained their spirits.

With Devizes becoming a permanent camp, plans had to be formulated in case there was an escape. Colonel Upton, the camp commandant, requested a meeting with the police to help plan for just such an eventuality. Consequently, on 29 September 1944 he had a meeting with Inspector Hector Shears of the Wiltshire Constabulary, based in the town. Inspector Shears' report stated:

On Friday, September 29th, at the request of the prisoner of war camp commandant, Col. Upton, I visited the P. of W. Camp together with

Major Copland-Griffiths, the local Officer Commanding the Home Guard. Col. Upton wished to contact myself and the Home Guard regarding arrangements to be made to deal with a situation arising in the event of a Prisoner of War escaping.

At the present moment there are between 5,000 and 6,000 prisoners of war in the camp, I cannot say how many will be stationed but possibly the greater portion of the present number will remain there. The staff at the camp has been reduced to almost a minimum, and I was informed that they are responsible for the prisoners whilst in the cage. As soon as they escape, the responsibility moves to the civil police, assisted by the Home Guard for the [re]capture of the prisoners.

I informed Col. Upton of the procedure on the report of prisoners escaping. It would be passed to the Chief Constable's Office, and immediately all Divisions would be contacted, if possible, at the same time, and the information circulated to them. In addition, if the escape had just occurred, then every effort locally would be made by the police in order to effect their [re]capture.[4]

The following day Inspector Shears attended a conference of local Home Guard officers on the same subject. His report went on to state:

They were very anxious to prepare schemes in order to assist in case they were required.

At the present moment, duty with the Home Guard is on a purely voluntary basis; it is not possible to detail a Platoon or a Company to stand by as in the past.

I explained to the company that I was of the opinion that two schemes would be required, one to deal with a small number of escapees, and the other to deal with a large break-out.

They agreed to the suggestion, and it was agreed to prepare a scheme to deal with a break-out of up to five prisoners, and one to deal with a break-out of more than five prisoners.

A conference of all Home Guard officers is being held on Monday, October 2nd, in order to prepare details for the proposed schemes, and to contact the members of the Home Guard in order to obtain the names of the personnel who would be prepared to volunteer for this duty.[5]

The meeting went on to discuss just how the Home Guard would be notified in the event of a break-out and there appears to have been much discussion centred around the use of a loudspeaker van held by the police. At the same time, matters became more complicated as regards the employment of the Home Guard in such a way. On 7 October 1944 the Commanding Officer of the 4th Wiltshire Home Guard battalion wrote to the Chief Constable, Lieutenant-Colonel Sir Hoel Llewellyn KBE, DSO, DL, thus:

> Officer Commanding 'D' (Devizes) Company informs this Headquarters that he has been requested by Inspector Shears to stand-by in the event of trouble arising with Prisoners of War.
>
> Will you kindly advise whether you are likely to call on the Home Guard in which case, will you be good enough to make an official request for such assistance so that Higher Authorities may be approached for sanction for the payment of Compensation for Loss of earnings, Injuries sustained (if any) and Subsistence allowance in the event of a turn-out. Is the assistance of outlying companies likely to be required in view of the very small area controlled by 'D' Company?
>
> The Home Guard will be most willing to assist in any way within their power in what appears likely to prove a most serious situation.[6]

On 11 October the Chief Constable duly requested formal assistance in the event of an escape and there the matter rested.

As autumn marched on into winter, an uneasiness descended over many of the permanent POW Camps in Britain. The prisoners were becoming restless. The incidence of individual escapes from camps and absconding from work parties was on the increase. As yet, very few large-scale escapes had been attempted. Suddenly, however, reports started to come into the War Office that prisoners were escaping, or attempting to escape, from camps all over the country. Reports were being circulated both to the local police constabularies and Home Commands on a regular basis. One such report arrived at Devizes and amply demonstrates how unprepared the country was, as a whole, to deal with escaping prisoners. It described the *modus operandi* of three German *Luftwaffe* prisoners who attempted to escape to Ireland from a camp in the north of England:

RESTRICTED

> Herman LANGE
> Thedor HOLZ
> Herman AHRENDT

At about 22.00 hours on 17 November 1944 the above-named German

PW escaped through the perimeter wire of 184 PW Camp. They were recaptured at HOLYHEAD whilst attempting to board a steamer for EIRE on the afternoon of 23 November 1944. During the night of 17/18 November 1944, the PW walked to CHEPSTOW. At the time one was wearing *Luftwaffe* trousers and a leather jacket, another was wearing dark blue trousers and a knee-length drab wind-jacket with zip fasteners, and the third was wearing complete *Luftwaffe* uniform without badges. One PW could speak poor French and fair English, by no means fluent or free from accent; another could speak very little English indeed; the third could speak only German.[7]

The report went on to describe how the prisoners had changed a French 1,000 franc note at a branch of Barclays Bank in Chepstow. They had then bought train tickets to Gloucester where they changed for Birmingham. Meeting two military policemen, they were directed to a Service Club for the night. Running short of cash, Lange sold his watch to the owner of a fish and chip shop for twelve pounds which enabled them to take the train to Liverpool, where they spent two nights in the YMCA hostel. In Liverpool the escapees bought second hand clothing – exempt from coupons – and then bought tickets for a passage to Dublin, posing as French volunteers who had been ordered to report to the French Consul there. The report went on to say:

Their 'passports' or 'Identity Documents', which were made whilst in the camp, were poor specimens. The 'stamp' was produced by placing a French franc under the card and taking a rubbing. PW stated they showed these documents repeatedly to police, at 'Soldiers' Homes' etc., and they were always accepted when they put on a bold front.

They had stated that they walked about the streets of all the towns they visited. They spent periods in railway trains, public houses and restaurants, all without the slightest interference. They said they were surprised at the friendliness of the English, the quality of the food and the efficiency of the country's transport.[8]

Then, on 18 and 19 November 1944 the camp staff at Devizes discovered that they, too, had had several escapes. Unlike others, however, the Devizes escape would lead to the discovery of a much larger plan. Like all other camps throughout the country, Camp 23 had a few prisoners who had been classified as 'Blacks'. The camp mostly held 'Greys', with a few 'Whites' who had been selected for such jobs as department interpreters and cookhouse fatigues in Le Marchant Barracks and the two American hospitals opposite. When the recaptured Germans were returned to the camp several days later, they were found to be a mixture of 'Blacks' and 'Greys', with a variety of reasons for making their escapes in the first place. It was to lead to a much greater scare.

As has already been noted by Dick Hurn, the Devizes staff had expected all along that escape attempts would be made. Purely by chance, alongside Captain Craig and Staff Sergeant Reis, the two British camp 'intelligence' personnel, there were also present several American Intelligence Officers from the 18th US Airborne Corps who were enhancing their interrogation techniques and language abilities, by practising on the German prisoners as real examples. Once the escapees had been returned to Devizes after several days on the run, these men began questioning them. What they discovered necessitated the immediate involvement of PWIS(H). In a series of reports prepared by Colonel Scotland and two of his staff, only recently released into the public domain, the initial escapes were described in detail. They discovered that the escapes had not been coordinated and by pure coincidence at the same time several groups had literally slipped away unnoticed. Perhaps the most successful group included Joachim Engel, a German senior NCO.

Engel was born in Berlin in 1922. Leaving school when only fourteen years old, he became an apprentice boy in the Works Department for the German state railways, based in Schoneweide. Called up in March 1940, he had served on both the eastern and western fronts with a variety of assault gun units. He had been captured at Lille, in northern France, on 3 September 1944. On arrival in England, Engel had spent four weeks at a camp near Bourton-on-the-Hill in Gloucestershire and then had been transferred to Devizes on 30 October 1944. In their report PWIS(H)/LDC/552, Scotland and his team described Engel as 'highly intelligent, well-spoken and possessed by a big "conscience"'. They described in detail how Engel appeared to regard himself as having acted in a cowardly fashion when captured as he still had ammunition available when he surrendered. He had already made two attempts to escape from captivity, but both had failed. PWIS(H) went on to note 'he is very sincere, and his statements are regarded as truthful'.[9] Describing Engel's escape, Scotland wrote:

PW left the camp on 18 Nov 44 together with O'Gefr [Corporal] Bruno KLOTH, O'Gefr Karl-Heinz ZASHE, Gefr Ernst KREBS and O'Gefr Herbert NIERENKOTER. The escape had been planned for a week, awaiting favourable weather, but the only instruments used were wooden sticks to hold apart the wire. No rations or other materials were taken. Two other men only had knowledge of their venture, O'Gefr GESSER and O'Gefr GOENIG, who were told immediately before the escape.

Scotland went on to describe their time out of the camp and how they so nearly succeeded in reaching freedom:

PW left A-1 Compound through the wire, crossed the tented camp, crossed the two roads and then kept a course parallel to the main road. By the time morning came they had lost their way and spent the day in an empty sheep pen near a small town. During the next night [19/20 November] they reached an aerodrome, about eight miles from this camp. They remained hiding in bushes until the following evening to observe; they came to the conclusion that it was an aerodrome used only by training planes. The following night [21 November] they succeeded in entering two planes, but the engines were cold and would not start up. They felt cold and wet, had eaten nothing except turnips and berries for two days, and finally decided to give themselves up. This they did next morning [22 November] in a nearby village.

PW stated that both one of his comrades, who had been a glider pilot, and he himself had hoped to be able to pilot a plane. He also said that though he himself was supposed to be in charge of the expedition, there was continual squabbling going on about which way to take and where to spend the day.

The airfield that Engel and his fellow travellers reached was RAF Yatesbury, nestled just below the Marlborough Downs. The fact that they penetrated the airfield and were able to attempt to steal two aircraft must have been supremely embarrassing for the authorities, for Yatesbury was more than just a flying school.

RAF Yatesbury dated back to the Royal Flying Corps in 1917. Located 4½ miles east of Calne, in 1944 it housed three training schools as part of 27 Training Group, RAF. Alongside a basic flying school – the Bristol Flying School using Tiger Moth aircraft – Yatesbury also housed No. 2 Radio School and the highly secret No. 9 Radio School which incorporated No. 1 Radar Wing, specialising in training RAF ground radar operators. Security was described as 'tight' by many who were there during the war but few ever knew that four German prisoners of war had successfully managed to climb aboard two aircraft. One man who did know was Flying Officer Alfred Daltry. He wrote:

> I was a young pilot stationed at No. 2 RFS [Radio Flying School] Yatesbury from June 1944 until January 1945. One morning at breakfast we were told that flying was cancelled for the day due to an 'incident' during the night. Some escaping German POWs from nearby Devizes had got two of our little Percivals out of a hangar [but] failed to get them airborne (all grass – no runways).
>
> We pilots welcomed the excitement as a relief from the monotonous daily grind of piloting the planes while our cadet passengers (one in a Proctor, two in a Preceptor) carried out wireless operating air-to-ground exercises.
>
> Whilst an influx of military security personnel searched around for the POWs, and for any evidence of sabotage, we youngsters returned to the mess to discuss the incident between hands of poker or bridge – the normal pastime when unable to fly.
>
> We assumed that the escapees were pilots and we considered that their failure to start the planes' engines was understandable because engine starting was a disciplined, but simple, procedure carried out by the pilot and ground staff using a mobile heavy-duty power supply.
>
> We disagreed, however, about whether or not the Germans were capable of sussing out the planes' controls in the dark and flying off into the night. We were told later, the next day I believe, that three POWs had given themselves up in the nearby village of Cherhill and no signs of sabotage had been discovered anywhere, and so, for me, it was back to the daily flying chore.[10]

Alice Grant was a WAAF teleprinter operator at Yatesbury. Now living in Malmesbury, she also recalls the incident all those years ago:

> At that time I was a WAAF teleprinter operator at Yatesbury camp and remember the [POW] camp . . . as when off duty friends and myself used to pass the camp when cycling into Devizes; an arduous trip but we used to enjoy it.
>
> Prior to the 'Devizes Plot' there was a break-out by four prisoners,

recaptured by one of our officers, Squadron Leader 'Spud' Murphy, on his way to camp at 7.30 in the morning. This was by the Black Horse pub at Cherhill. Security became exceedingly tight at our camp after that, as we were No. 2 Flying School for Aircrew Signals personnel, with Tiger Moths at the Flying School. Both were an opportunity for any prisoner to make an attempt to get away.[11]

Engels and his co-escapees were not the only prisoners to visit RAF Yatesbury. Two others had also passed that way on the night of 19 November 1944. The two prisoners concerned, SS Oberscharführer Beier and Feldwebel Westermann, gave a strange reason for their escape – apparently they both wanted to get to America!

Beier was only twenty-two when he made his escape. A civilian clerk in peacetime, he had been born in Berlin. PWIS(H) described him as 'fairly educated and . . . an unpleasant type of young Nazi'. In France Beier had apparently become separated from his unit. He had then decided to go to America and commandeered an army truck, intent on driving to the Spanish border. He had been arrested by the French Police while driving south! Westermann in turn had been an agricultural fitter before joining the *Wehrmacht*. Aged thirty, married with one child, he was described as 'quiet and unintelligent, and it is felt that he would not have given any trouble had it not been for Beier's influence'. PWIS(H) went on to describe in their report that Beier had had for many years an urge to emigrate to the States, as his parents and sister were dead. While in Devizes he had requested several times to be allowed to join up in the American Army and fight the Japanese in order to obtain US citizenship. On being refused, he had persuaded Westermann to join him in an attempt to escape to America, either by stowing away in an aeroplane or on board ship.

Both Beier and Westermann escaped from Devizes on the night of 19 November 1944. Colonel Scotland's PWIS(H) stated:

About 1930 hrs on 19th Nov 44 both PW met at Cookhouse II and broke camp by way of the 'Overflow' Compound. They crossed the road leading along the camp and then followed the main road to the far end of the American Hospital camps. From there they went across country and climbed a hill, where they hid in a wooden shack from 2230 hrs until the afternoon of 20 Nov. Next evening they continued in the direction of an aerodrome which they had located by its lights and by seeing aircraft land and take off. They crossed another hill surmounted by a monument [probably the Lansdown Monument] and descended into the valley beyond, where they found a road fringed by houses. By this time they felt cold and hungry – having eaten nothing except some turnips – and both men were footsore. They had only seen training planes take off from the airfield and despaired of their chance to reach America. So they returned to camp by the way they had come, attempting to re-enter their compound unseen; but they were noticed and arrested when already inside the camp grounds.[12]

Interestingly enough, it seems that no official records referring to these incidents at Yatesbury have survived. Neither the RAF Station Log nor the Log of No. 9 Radio School make any mention of the POW visit. Nor do the War Diaries of Southern Command or SPDD. It is almost as if the authorities were embarrassed to the point of total exclusion over the incident.

The PWIS(H) interrogators also revealed some facts that were to lead to some very wild rumours the following month. For, while out, Beier and Westermann chanced on a fortunate discovery. The Scotland report again:

At about 1700 hrs on 20 Nov, PW spent some time in a glasshouse, the door of which they found open, belonging to a hatter named PRITCHARD ex Devizes. Amongst other articles of furniture this glasshouse contained a chest of drawers, in which they looked for food and a torch. WESTERMANN only found a file, which he kept, but BEIER discovered some detonators and a length of fuse in one of the drawers. He asked WESTERMANN what they should do with them. WESTERMANN, however, claims to have seen the fuse only and replied that this stuff was useless, and these articles were left where they had been found.[13]

Two other prisoners also escaped during the night of 19 November; Unteroffizier Rolf Herzig and Kanonier Gunther Rese. Little is known today of this escape. The PWIS(H) report only briefly states that they escaped on the same night as Beier and Westermann, only to give themselves up the following day.

As can be imagined, the camp staff were thoroughly alarmed that so many individual escapes were taking place simultaneously. And since the escapes had only been discovered the following morning the prisoners had had some time to put distance between themselves and the camp and any immediate follow-up action by the local police and/or Home Guard. Reports were also coming in from other camps of the same type of activity. What was going on and why?

CHAPTER SEVEN

A Daring Plot

No escape story of the Second World War was more
daring, more fantastic, more ambitious, more hopelessly
fanatical than that of the prisoners of Devizes.
                              Lieutenant-Colonel A.P. Scotland[1]

One of the most important staff appointments in a POW camp is that
of Senior Interpreter. One of his tasks is to keep the Commandant
fully briefed on the moods and goings-on within his camp. Captain
Craig held this appointment in Devizes. Little is known about
Captain Craig except that he was badged Royal Artillery, like the
Adjutant, Captain Hurn. According to Robert Jackson's book *A Taste
of Freedom* Craig was a 'dark lean Gunner who had been to school in
Switzerland'.[2] Alongside Craig was the German refugee, Staff
Sergeant Reis. The latter had been a publisher in Stuttgart before
coming to this country in the late Thirties. Like many of his fellow
refugees, he had been interned on the Isle of Man and had
subsequently volunteered to join the Pioneer Corps. He then found
himself at Devizes, battling against a badly deteriorating situation.

According to Dick Hurn, Captain Craig was very good at his job.
More importantly, he had set up a system of stool-pigeons – 'Whites'
– who would tell him every detail of what was happening on a daily
basis. Dick Hurn recalls:

> Craig was a key man. He had organised his stool pigeons – his 'stoolies' –
> so that he had one or two in each compound. All of them were doing jobs
> around the camp and were reporting directly to Craig and Reis. This was
> very effective as we didn't have any microphones and so on.[3]

One of Craig's more useful 'stoolies' was a conscripted Ukrainian,
Petar Urlicher. He and others were urged to try to discover what was
going on inside the various compounds. With nine prisoners already

out, Craig and the camp commandant Colonel Upton were also forced to inform their higher command at Headquarters Salisbury Plain District, and so it went up the chain. It is interesting to note that neither command recorded the November escapes in their War Diaries nor is there any record in the Wiltshire Constabulary radio log or daily reports. It would seem that all the local authorities had been caught unawares by events, a reasonable claim when seen in the light of what was to transpire within a month.

On 20 November Urlicher informed Craig that a prisoner called Hermann Storch was planning to escape. Storch was duly placed in detention as PWIS(H) recorded later:

> Just after the break, i.e. on 20 Nov, STORCH was placed in detention together with the escapers not because he had participated but because he was reported to the camp authorities by an informer who knew that he was preparing an individual escape, possibly with two other PW.
>
> He was found to be in possession of a compass (received from a man whose Christian name was HENRY in A-1 Compound), a sketch lent him for copying by a Studienprofessor (unidentified) and a large kitchen knife. STORCH intended to escape with two other PW, Christian names PAUL and KARL, neither of whom had definitely undertaken to accompany him.[4]

Hermann Storch was regarded by all concerned with some disdain. He had already attempted to escape twice from a camp in Scotland where, alongside a *Luftwaffe* prisoner, he had planned to steal an aircraft and fly it back to Germany. This plan had been thwarted when security at the camp was tightened after another escape attempt. He was also known to spread the most outlandish rumours. Again in Scotland, the story that the liner *Queen Mary*, full of German prisoners on their way to America, had been intercepted by Japanese submarines and escorted to a Norwegian port, was attributed to Storch. On being placed in detention at Devizes alongside recaptured prisoners, Storch was later joined by further prisoners. Two of these were SS Unterscharführer Joachim Goltz and SS Grenadier Kurt Zühlsdorff. These two were 'Blacks' of the highest order who had been caught trying to leave their compound on the night of 26 November. Under questioning they revealed that they had intended to break into the rations store of the American

128th General Hospital in Waller Barracks. This had been Goltz's third such escape in as many weeks. On one occasion, Goltz claimed, he had simply walked out of the front gate when the guards had not been watching too closely.

Goltz had been only sixteen when he joined the SS in 1941. He must have impressed his recruiters for he was sent to the élite 1st SS Panzer Division 'Leibstandarte Adolf Hitler' (1LAH). Wherever the fighting was toughest, this division was there. Virtually destroyed at the battle of Kharkov during the Kursk Offensive in 1943, the division had been transferred to northern Italy to reform as a panzer (tank) division. Immediately after the Normandy landings, 1 LAH moved north to France and was involved in the failed Mortain counter-attack against the Americans. Withdrawing under extreme pressure after Patton's Third Army broke out, the division was again destroyed inside the Falaise Pocket. It was here that Goltz had been captured.

Kurt Zühlsdorff's story was very similar to Goltz's. A grocer's assistant before the war, he had also joined the SS and was posted to the 17th SS Panzer Grenadier Division, named after an infamous German robber-baron of the Middle Ages, Gotz von Berchlingen. The 17th SS was a relatively new division, having been formed in late 1943 in western France. Unlike the original SS divisions, manpower shortages meant that the new division had had to accept many non-German recruits, especially Belgians and Rumanians. On 6 June 1944 the 17th SS was south of Tours in a reserve role. Rushed north, it first entered action on 11 June around Carentan where it came into contact with the American 82nd and 101st Airborne Divisions. By late July the divisional remnants were fighting a withdrawal action around St Lo and were subsequently reported by the German 7th Army as having ceased to exist.[5] Zühlsdorff had been forced to surrender along with others at about that time.

Both Goltz and Zühlsdorff were pure Nazis. They had known nothing else. Consequently, their belief in Hitler and the Party was absolute. Zühlsdorff also carried some sort of a grudge: he claimed that while in France, he had been held by the Maquis for a time. Whether this was true cannot be determined, but it was to drive him to murder only a month later.

It appears, from all the available records, that Storch was not questioned straightaway. He had been put into detention on 20 November and was joined by Goltz and Zühlsdorff on the 26th. It was only when all three were together that questioning started. Storch himself was questioned by Lieutenant Voegeli, one of the American Intelligence Officers on attachment. It seemed to be a tremendous opportunity for those under training – a real situation, looking for real answers. Little did they know what would eventually transpire. The interrogation report on Storch stated:

> This officer [Voegeli] was not satisfied with STORCH's explanation that he had no connection with the recent escape of the PW and accused him directly of being the instigator of the break of 19/20 Nov, who had not gone with the main party so as not to attract attention to himself. The seriousness of such a charge was made quite clear to STORCH and he took fright.[6]

Hermann Storch did a lot more than take fright. He started to reveal a most audacious plot for the whole camp of some 7,500 prisoners to break out. To begin with, Storch revealed that the prisoner Beier had discovered some detonators on his trip outside the wire, and that he had heard from the SS man Goltz that a plan was well under way, organised by another prisoner called Wunderlich. He claimed that Wunderlich was really a *Luftwaffe* officer, not the lowly corporal he appeared to be. He claimed that he had been told by Goltz that Wunderlich was in contact with two 'agents' – both British soldiers – outside the camp whom he had met while on a work detail. Contact had been made with Germany through these agents and their secret wireless. Storch claimed that Wunderlich had organised a break-out from the camp which would be assisted by an airborne drop from Germany. Once out, the prisoners would form themselves into battle groups and storm nearby barracks to obtain transport and weapons. They would then march east, attacking what they believed was a local tank depot. Continuing on their way, they would try to reach the east coast around the Wash in East Anglia where they would be taken off by waiting ships.

The plan was to be activated on 24 December at 7 p.m. and was to be known as 'Die Dritter Front' (the Third Front). The start of the operation was to be signalled verbally using the word 'Hummelkose', the recognition of which was to be acknowledged using the reply 'Erika'. (For some undiscovered reason this was later changed to 'Koln'.) Throughout the operation, the password 'Hans Drei – Gustav Vier' was to be used, safely identifying fellow plotters. Lieutenant Voegeli's reaction on hearing such a story can only be imagined!

Colonel Upton was duly informed and was left with no choice but to report everything the American interrogators had discovered. On orders from MI19, Colonel Scotland at PWIS(H) hurriedly dispatched two of his interrogators from the London Cage to Devizes soon after. Dick Hurn again:

> Colonel Scotland's boys, two or three of them, came down from London. They were very impressive and could have a prisoner in tears in ten minutes. We had them with us for a long time. At the same time, we were being advised by the Headquarters at Salisbury Plain District. They also sent down one or two staff officers who were useless.[7]

Unfortunately, the officers from London were not identified in the subsequent reports but their efforts in getting to the bottom of what became a most serious threat have survived the shredder. While the PWIS(H) officers got themselves organised, the American interrogators continued to question those who had initially escaped. So far, Storch had implicated Wunderlich as the leader and chief organiser of the plot. Here the Americans made a mistake. They may not have believed the whole story, but they did seem to believe that Wunderlich was the leader. Consequently, they sought and received permission to put Storch into the Navy and *Luftwaffe* compound, A-3, where he could continue to monitor Wunderlich's planning and report back on a daily basis through the stool-pigeon network. Scotland's officers must have agreed with this and soon a daily ritual developed. Dick Hurn again:

> After the [November] escapes, it all started to come out. We heard about a mass break-out which was supposed to join up with other camps. We also heard that this was to be combined with an air drop from Germany. Every evening, after dinner, we all used to meet in the Colonel's office for a sit. rep. from the intelligence officers. This had to be after the prisoners

had been locked up for the night in case they suspected we were on to them. By then, of course, we had put up triple wire fences and carbide lighting. Later we introduced guard dogs and handlers. We hadn't had these before.[8]

At this point in the story, it is worth considering just how difficult a situation the authorities faced. Here was a plan, in the heart of southern England, that envisaged several thousand escaped German prisoners with airborne support, fighting their way to the east coast and being taken off by a German armada of ships. It was crazy, yet plausible. At the same time, although unknown to the camp staff in Devizes, there was also some intelligence evidence that backed up the idea of German support.

On 25 October 1944 the German High Command had issued an order requesting all units to put forward volunteers for a very special operation. This message was subsequently retransmitted to every major command, including the Armeekorps in operational charge of firing V2s from Holland. With such widespread distribution, this message was inevitably intercepted and decoded at Bletchley Park. Indeed a complete translation appeared in the Intelligence Summary of 30 November 1944, published by the First Canadian Army, then fighting to form several bridgeheads over the River Waal in Holland. It read:

The Führer has ordered the formation of a special unit of a strength of about two battalions for employment on reconnaissance and special duties on the Western Front. The personnel will be assembled from volunteers of all arms of the Army and Waffen-SS who must fulfil the following requirements:

a) Physically A-1, suitable for special tasks, mentally keen, strong personality.

b) Fully trained in single [hand-to-hand] combat.

c) Knowledge of the English language and also the American dialect. Especially important is a knowledge of military technical terms.

This order is to be made known immediately to all units and headquarters. Volunteers may not be retained on military grounds but are to be sent immediately to Friedenthal near Oranienburg (Headquarters Skorzeny) for a test of suitability.

The volunteers that do not pass these tests satisfactorily will be returned to their headquarters and units. The volunteers are to report to Friedenthal by November 10 latest.

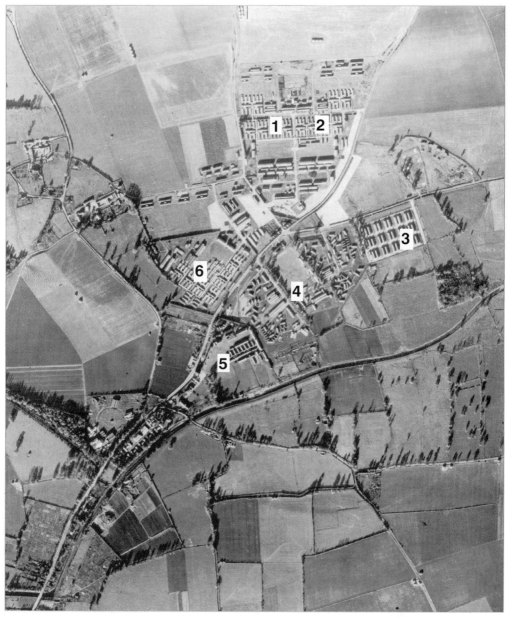

The Devizes camp area, 1946. (Photo: RCHME)

1. Waller Barracks
2. Prince Maurice Barracks
3. PoW Camp Romney huts
4. Le Marchant Camp
5. Le Marchant Barracks
6. Hopton Barracks

German prisoners of war awaiting onward transportation from Southampton, 8 June 1944. (Photo: IWM H39265)

German prisoners boarding a train for Kempton Park, 8 June 1994. (Photo: IWM H39269)

Le Marchant Barracks, c. *1910.*

Le Marchant Barracks, 1996. (Photo: Author)

The remarkable Daily Express *photograph of Camp 23, Devizes. It was probably taken on 17 December 1944, the day after the prisoner arrests. (Photo:* Daily Express*)*

The same scene in 1996. (Photo: Author)

These Romney huts are all that remain of Camp 23, Devizes. Re-skinned in the late 1980s, they now house part of the County Council Highways Department. (Photo: Author)

Once there were 700 prisoners here — now there are only council signs and stores. (Photo: Author)

These photographs were probably taken at Kempton Park on 8 June 1944. Note the similarity of the tower in the background to that at Le Marchant Barracks. (Photos: IWM H39275 and IWM H39273)

'Charlie' May, Devizes, 1945.
(Photo: 'Charlie' May)

Edith Ockenden, née Fletcher,
was an LACW at RAF
Yatesbury in 1944. (Photo:
Mr & Mrs Ockenden)

Captain Dick Hurn, Adjutant at Camp 23, Devizes, photographed with some of the orderly room staff in 1945. (Photo: Dick Hurn)

128 (US) General Hospital in Waller Barracks, in the winter of 1944/5. (Photo: Author via Walter Chebatoris)

Some of the staff of 128 (US) General Hospital on parade at Waller Barracks in 1945.

Waller Barracks in 1996. (Photo: Author)

These two photographs show the initial searching and interrogation of German prisoners in June 1944. (Photos: IWM H39270 and IWM H39276)

Officers of B Company, 8th Para; left to right: Lieutenant Cox, Major Kippin, Lieutenant Dudley. (Photo: Author via Frank Ockenden)

Men of B Company, 8th Para. Frank Ockenden is in the middle row, his arms resting on the shoulders of his comrades. (Photo: Author via Frank Ockenden)

Lieutenant (now Colonel) Alistair Wilson, 6th Airborne Armoured Reconnaissance Regiment. (Photo: A. Wilson)

Bandsman Arthur McKechnie, The Wiltshire Regiment. (Photo: A. McKechnie)

The band of the 2nd Battalion, The Wiltshire Regiment, photographed at Le Marchant Barracks in 1945. Note the American trucks in the background.

The band playing for the resident Americans at Le Marchant Barracks in 1945.

Captain Wheatley (front row, left) and other JAG officers in the winter of 1943. (Photo: John Wheatley)

Even today, evidence of German prisoners can be found in and around Devizes. This is a German dog-tag, which once belonged to a member of Landschutzen Kompanie 80 from Military Area VI, based at Münster. (Photo: John Winchcombe)

Doug Richards, Welsh Guards,
1945. (Photo: D. Richards)

Doug Richards today,
photographed in the former
London Cage in 1995.
(Photo: D. Richards)

Lieutenant-Colonel Archibald Wilson, Commandant of Camp 21, Comrie, Scotland. (Photo: Liverpool Constabulary)

The Reichsführer-SS [Himmler] will inform OKW/WFSt by November 12 of the number of volunteers who have been tested and the number who were accepted after these tests, these figures being broken down for each branch of the *Wehrmacht*.[9]

We now know that this message referred to a planned operation to insert German special forces behind the Allied lines during the Ardennes Offensive which burst upon the Americans on 16 December 1944. The volunteers were formed into a new unit called 'Panzerbrigade-150'. This was commanded by the now infamous SS-Obersturmbannführer Otto Skorzeny, the man who had rescued Mussolini from his mountain-top prison using a small force of paratroops landed by glider.

In November 1944, of course, the Allies suspected nothing as regards the Ardennes Offensive. Indeed it was perhaps one of the more important intelligence failures of the war. Then, out of the blue, a plan was suddenly revealed whereby a massive escape of prisoners of war was to be supported by a parachute drop. Could the intercepted message from the German High Command refer to just such a plan? Dick Hurn remembers at the time that this was very much what people thought, adding urgency to the determination to discover what was really going on. He went on to say:

The real crunch came when the prisoners started issuing 'Orders of the Day'. The intelligence officers managed to get a copy. One of these stated that the 'day had almost arrived'. We had been warned about a possible airborne drop and we knew we had to move fairly swiftly. The District Headquarters ordered a local parachute battalion to come and surround the camp so we could pounce on the ringleaders.

On 14 December it was decided that the move against the plot should start: the authorities had learned that the plan had been brought forward to start on 16 December. Dick Hurn again:

The Para officers came and did a recce and we planned to move at about 9.30/10.00 p.m. A company of paras arrived but did not move into the camp, just surrounded it. With them came a number of coaches and I had also been warned that a tank might be used but it never appeared as far as I can remember. The prisoners were terrified of the Paras when they recognised their red berets.

Then a bugle sounded and the whole camp was paraded. I and Reis then went into each compound in turn and called out two or three names in each. These men were then escorted out to the waiting coaches and driven off to the London Cage. That was the last we saw of them. Within twenty-four hours, the place was in uproar![10]

The first 'Order of the Day' was issued on 12 December. It had been written in Wunderlich's handwriting but signed by Storch. It read:

Order of the Day No. 1

Men of the Freedom Movement.
The hour of our liberation has approached and it is the duty of every German to fight once more, arms in hand, against World Jewry.
I demand of every German man to fight for his Fatherland without hesitation.
It is the duty of every leader of the Freedom Movement to fight as a German and not wage the fight for liberation like a plunderer and murderer.
I call upon and demand of all men to stand by their colours faithfully and bravely.

STORCH[11]

On the same day, Storch issued his first 'situation report'. Again it had been written by Wunderlich.

General Situation

1. Utmost secrecy in every respect.
2. Honourable fighting and tenacious holding-on.
3. Everyone will be held responsible who offends against discipline and international law; severe punishment will be imposed in such cases.
4. Plunder, theft and similar offences will be punishable by execution.
5. The leaders will be responsible to put up fighting groups, each of the strength of a company of 150/180 men; these will be sub-divided into platoons and sections.

STORCH[12]

The plot was certainly taken seriously. For December 1944 the War Diary of the Headquarters of the Salisbury Plain and Dorset District recorded the following:

23 PW Camp, Devizes
On 8 Dec, a US Interrogation team from XVIII Airborne Corps, working in Devizes camp, discovered what was reputed to be a large scale plot of the German PsW to break out. A PW named STORCH was the informer.

The break was timed for Xmas eve or New Year's Eve when a relaxation on the part of guards etc. was hoped for. In broad outline the plot was to overpower all guards, seize all arms in the Camp, Le Marchant Barracks and at 141 and 128 US General Hospitals, all of which adjoin. Some 50 to 60 vehicles were to be obtained at the two hospitals, where also a food store was known to be located. Army personnel, including Panzer elements, were to seize a large US tank depot in the vicinity, whilst GAF personnel proceeded in the captured lorries to a nearby training airfield. The training aircraft were to be seized and to be used in an attack on the nearest operational airfield. The first suitable a/c was to be flown straight to Germany, where two Airborne Divs were waiting in Holland ready to be dropped in support of the PsW. The whole was then to develop into an attack on LONDON.[13]

It was no wonder that the British authorities were alarmed. If local HQs were believing the accounts and information being fed to them by Storch, presumably agreed by the PWIS(H) interrogators, then it is likely that the information was considered genuine even higher up the chain of command. Worse was yet to follow. The War Diary again:

The ringleader, Ob.Gefr. WUNDERLICH, was alleged to be in contact with two German agents in the camp in British uniform, one a Staff Sgt and the other a Cpl. STORCH was a well educated and very logical man, whom interrogators suspected of being an officer in the guise of an OR.

The plot was reported to S [Southern] Command and two British Interrogators from MI19 were sent to the camp. By 14 Dec they had convinced themselves that STORCH's information was genuine and had obtained the names of the ringleaders. It was then discovered that the escape date had been advanced to 14 or 15 Dec and permission was obtained to break up the whole scheme. Accordingly, the 30 ringleaders were moved to the LDC [London District Cage] on the evening on the 14 Dec.[14]

Prior to the operation to detain the plotters, Southern Command ordered other measures just in case:

Precautionary measures taken were:
(a) 187 PW Camp, forming in Devizes, were moved into Le Marchant Bks on 10 Dec.

(b) One Coy 30 Devons, located at PORTLAND, were placed at 48 hrs notice to move to Le Marchant Bks, DEVIZES in an emergency. On 14 Dec this notice was shortened to 12 hrs.

(c) 6 A/B Div placed one Para Sqn, with one A/B Armd Recce Tp under comd, at 6 hrs notice on 12 Dec. This force was moved to the vicinity of the PW Camp during the afternoon of 14 Dec and was called into the camp during the arrest and removal of the ring-leaders.

(d) US Tps. As a result of information reaching XVIII Airborne Corps, US Southern Dist made call on US Field Tps, and task forces were 'alerted' for employment in support of certain US Depots in this and other Dists.[15]

The paratroop company detailed to assist in the breaking up of the plot was B Company from the 8th Parachute Battalion, known as 8 Para. They were stationed just outside Tilshead in the centre of Salisbury Plain. 8 Para had forged themselves a worthy reputation as part of the 6th Airborne Division and had jumped in the early hours of 6 June to secure the Allied left (eastern) flank prior to the main Normandy landings. Returning to England several months later, they had not been committed at Arnhem and by this time were in training for a number of possible future operations including, ultimately, the Rhine Crossing. On 2 December the battalion went on leave, having just finished training in Birmingham where they had been practising street-fighting in the bombed-out parts of the city. At the same time, they had also been warned-off to move from Tilshead to Corsham. In fact, the battalion advance party was due to move on 14 December, with the main battalion body moving on the 16th. B Company, then commanded by Major Kippin, had been the last to complete the training in Birmingham and therefore was the last due to leave Tilshead.

As the District Headquarters War Diary stated, the para company was supported by the Reconnaissance (Recce) Troop from B Squadron of the 6th Airborne Armoured Reconnaissance Regiment (6 AARR). This unit was a trifle unusual as they flew their light tanks and armoured cars into battle in the massive Hamilcar gliders designed for just that purpose. Like 8 Para, 6 AARR had also landed in France on 6 June, deploying their Tetrarch light tanks and Jeep patrols straight from the gliders. 6 AARR noted in their War Diary the unusual task they were assigned that December:

12 Dec
Recce Tp B Sqn placed u/c Coy 8 PARA Bn and at 5 hrs' notice to proceed to Devizes to assist in dealing with suspected attempt at mass escape from POW Camp.

14 Dec
Tp placed at 1 hr's notice and moved to Tilshead and later Devizes. Escape attempt did not take place but tp assisted in restoring order after arrest of the ringleaders.[16]

Tony Leake, today Doctor Leake, had just been promoted to Lance Corporal in October 1944 when he returned to B Company, 8 Para, at Tilshead. He was one of those rushed to Devizes on 14 December:

The whole battalion went on leave from 2 to 11 December and on return were packing up for our move to a new camp at Corsham. Then on the afternoon of 14 December there was a flap on and 'B' Coy was rushed in trucks to the POW Camp at Devizes about ten miles away to deal with a possible break-out of the German POWs.

When we arrived the whole place was in darkness and we took up positions around the compounds. The prisoners were roaming menacingly inside the compounds making us feel very insecure as we could not see properly what was happening, although of course we were fully armed. Eventually the lighting came on again and order was restored. I do not think there were any shots fired at any time and none of the prisoners were found outside their compounds. I think we were only at the POW camp for about two hours before we returned to Tilshead.[17]

Jim Wheeler was a full corporal in 4 Platoon, B Company. He also recalled the Devizes incident:

I was born and bred in Calne, so knew the area well. B Company was the only sub-unit left in Tilshead Camp – 'Stalag Tilshead' we used to call it – as the remainder of the battalion had left for Corsham.

We were rushed to the Devizes POW camp as the staff were having trouble with the prisoners. They kept getting out! We had heard at the time that some of them had made it to RAF Upavon and RAF Netheravon. Our orders were to show ourselves as much as possible. After a while, selected prisoners were loaded onto waiting buses and driven off to London.

We were very disappointed that we could not 'blood' our young men – we even said we would cut the wire for them. Don't forget, only 13 out of 120 of the company had returned from France. We had had to march back into Tilshead in single file so as not to frighten the new lads.[18]

Interestingly, Jim Wheeler was to come across German prisoners again after the war. After demobilisation, he found a job at Wedhampton Manor and made use of German work details from Patney. 'They didn't like me much, I made them really work.'

Frank Ockenden, Tom Hopkins and Leonard Northover were members of 5 Platoon, B Company. Frank Ockenden knew the POW Camp well as he used to pass it quite often on his way to RAF Yatesbury to meet up with his WAAF girlfriend, Edith Fletcher, whom he later married. Equipped with two Bren machine guns, they were ordered up into one of the guard towers around the camp. Frank Ockenden vividly recalled that night:

> It was on the 14th, and led by recce armoured cars, that B Coy proceeded to the German POW camp just outside Devizes on the right hand side of the road . . . every afternoon I used to pass the camp on foot to meet my WAAF girlfriend who was stationed at RAF Yatesbury on the Calne road.
>
> We had only been back in England about two months after fighting in France, so our attitude to the Germans was to shoot first and ask questions afterwards. I will never forget that day, it rained and blew hard – never gave up till we returned to Tilshead . . . I think the Germans had better living conditions than us.
>
> [We] had arrived at the camp by truck. All you could hear was a bloody loud noise. Eventually the camp was flood-lit, not only by lights in the huts but also by head-lamps from army trucks and in those lights we saw troops giving cigarettes to the bloody Germans. So out we jumped, pushing the British troops to one side, got to the outer wire and what cigarettes we saw trod them down into the mud, so the [Germans] could not get them. One or two tried and got rifle butts down on their hands. No bloody German was going to smoke English cigarettes if we could not. The Lieutenant of 5 Platoon went by the name of Skidmore. [He] got our sergeant, Sergeant Yates, to put us three on a charge . . . for using unnecessary force. Skidmore had only just joined the battalion, never seen any fighting or dead mates left behind in Normandy. Company Sergeant-Major Markham told Sergeant Yates to forget the charge and said he would have a talk with our Major, J. Kippin, about it. It was later dropped.[19]

Tom Hopkins recalls the order to get into one of the guard towers:

> I remember doing the street fighting in Birmingham and then going on leave until being called back to camp not knowing why and ending up being escorted to the POW camp with Len Northover and Frank Ockenden. Major Kippin and Sergeant-Major Markham were in charge

who told us to go in the one tower with the Bren guns and, if necessary, if things turned nasty, to fire over the heads of the POWs. However, I think we ended up firing in front of them to stop them. Northover said something like he wished they would stop as they were unarmed and they did![20]

Both Tom Hopkins and Frank Ockenden recall that the prisoners did make a move towards the wire. The mayhem that was emerging must have started after the whole camp had been paraded and Dick Hurn was moving between compounds calling out the names. Frank Ockenden again:

The major told us that we may have to go into the camp, this we prayed and hoped would happen. On each corner . . . was a watch tower with two British troops armed with rifles. Kippin ordered them down and Northover, Hopkins and myself armed with two Bren guns took over with orders to fire over their heads if they did not get back from the wire. At least we had a roof over us even though we were wet through to the skin and cold. We had been up there for two hours when the [Germans] started up again, pushing up to the barbed wire. I myself was watching Major Kippin when his arm went down [and] I said to Tom Hopkins and Leonard 'fire over their heads'. They did not. They emptied four magazines across the front of their feet that stopped them dead in their tracks. After that some officers came up to the main gate and had a talk with the buggers. Then a platoon of Paras went in and the ringleaders were sorted out and later taken away to London.[21]

Peter Roberts was then Platoon Sergeant of 4 Platoon, commanded by Lieutenant Carden. His platoon had been the first to deploy at the camp that night:

On arrival at the camp, I recall seeing a lot of prisoners 'milling about' and a lot of noise coming from the compound. Lieutenant Carden went to consult a group of persons whom I assumed were camp officials and guards. He returned and instructed me to deploy the platoon in positions to contain a mass break-out. As my section commanders were taking their men to various positions, they were in full view of the camp inmates. One or two German prisoners, on seeing us, shouted to the other prisoners 'Englander Fallschirmjaeger'. The groups of prisoners then appeared to break up.

We remained in position for some considerable time. Nothing appeared to be happening . . . afterwards I was told that the authorities had regained full control of the camp; any prisoners 'armed' had been 'disarmed'. The trouble had ended. As one 'wag' commented 'it was our job to capture the Germans – not to look after them in POW Camps!'[22]

Harry Gosling, who now lives in Australia, was a member of 6 Platoon under Second Lieutenant Dudley. They were to provide the escorts on the coaches taking the ringleaders to the London Cage. He recalls the attitude of the prisoners:

We arrived at the POW camp and within a short while loaded the selected POWs on to a coach and delivered them to the London 'Cage' at Kensington Palace Gardens.

I must say we were afforded a great deal of respect by the POWs right from the beginning when we arrived to assist the guards in the segregation. There were some German paras among them who greeted us and I remember a few 'panzer' and *Luftwaffe* [prisoners].[23]

Alongside B Company, 8 Para, was the Recce troop from B Squadron, 6 AARR. Alastair Wilson, commissioned into the 17th/21st Lancers, was on attachment to the regiment and commanded the troop sent to Devizes. He, too, recalls with some clarity the night in question:

My regiment . . . had returned to Larkhill from Normandy in August 1944. Sometime in mid-December, I was told to draw G 1098 war stores and place my Troop at five hours' notice to move. I was to report to some headquarters in Tilshead wearing no Airborne insignia and in an unmarked vehicle.

We were briefed on an expected mass break-out at the POW camp at Devizes. About twelve officers inspected the Prison Camp, in the guise of a Sanitary Inspection Team. A further, more detailed, briefing was given by the Camp Commandant.

I returned to Larkhill to find my troop convinced that we were going off on some airborne mission. [The] troop consisted of two Daimler scout cars and two Bren Gun carriers. A day or two later, at about seven in the evening, we moved to Devizes to join the Paras at their debussing point. The Paras were in full battle order, but wearing gym shoes to avoid noise. The Paras marched to the camp and were deployed round the entire perimeter in total darkness. The POWs were then paraded and only then were all the lights switched on. My vehicles drove slowly round the perimeter with weapons trained on the surprised Germans. About thirty ringleaders were hauled from the ranks, put into buses and escorted to London.[24]

Two days after the arrest of the German ringleaders at Devizes, Hitler launched his last, desperate gamble to cut through the American lines and take Antwerp: Operation 'Wacht am Rhein', the Ardennes Offensive. On 16 December Skorzeny's English-speaking special forces slipped across behind the American lines and started to cause serious problems. They never were intended for a drop over southern England. The 8th Parachute Battalion was again quickly warned-off for an emergency deployment to the continent. They moved to Southampton between 17 and 19 December and were given their final orders at 9.30 p.m. on the 20th in Belgium. 6 AARR was also rushed out to the continent, deploying on 21 December. The German prisoners in Britain and elsewhere were overjoyed. For SS prisoners like Goltz and Zühlsdorff, now about to face some tough interrogations in London, 'Wacht am Rhein' really did appear to be the deliverance they had all longed for.

CHAPTER EIGHT

The Truth of the Matter

If I can deceive my own friends
I can make certain of deceiving the enemy.
General Thomas Jackson[1]

With the arrest of the ringleaders at Devizes on the night of 14 December 1944, the authorities could sleep somewhat more easily in their beds. In all, twenty-eight prisoners were removed to the London Cage, with a further four detained the next day and also taken to London. The uproar had been mostly contained within the immediate area. However, the initial scare had not gone totally unnoticed. Headquarters Salisbury Plain and Dorset District had notified various commands including the Americans. At the same time Dick Hurn alerted other local units, especially the two American General Hospitals in Waller and Prince Maurice Barracks opposite. Colonel 'Mac' Stilwell was visited twice with updates on what was taking place and he subsequently took the unusual step of ordering his officers and men, including the doctors and male nursing staff, to draw their personal weapons. Walter Chebatoris was one of those in 128 General Hospital:

> Our hospital, 128th General, was alerted to the escape. All officers and non-commissioned officers were issued side-arms. When we found out that the escape did not occur, the alert was over and everything went back to normal.[2]

Colonel Stilwell spent the whole evening of the 14th, according to Dick Hurn, standing guard at the front gate of his hospital, just in case!

Next door, Le Marchant Barracks was relatively empty. The only British soldiers there were the Wiltshire Regiment depot staff and the band of the 2nd Battalion. Sid Curry, who today lives in Coventry, was a member of the band:

We were told to draw out rifles and ammo and guard the upstairs windows of the married quarters block which we were in anyway. The band-boys' part was at the end next to the practice room. Everyone (except the boys) was armed including the 'pig-corporal' [who was in charge of the battalion sty] and the cooks. Some of the 'wide-boys' from London said they were non-combatants. Band Master Dalrymple ('Dally') threatened that he would send them to Burma! He was a much-feared man who allowed you to do what you liked providing you didn't get caught or bring the band into disrepute.

Anyway nothing happened to us and the next thing we knew was the tanks arriving [6 AARR] – they completely surrounded the camp. We also heard trucks with reinforcements.[3]

Despite the detailed planning by Inspector Shears of the Wiltshire Constabulary in Devizes, neither the police nor the Home Guard appear to have been involved. There is nothing in the records of either, including the verbatim radio log of the police. Dick Hurn confirmed that the police had not been involved as far as he could remember:

I do, however, remember seeing the police from Bishops Cannings around that time. They were worried about the behaviour of a lady who went by the nickname of 'Hay-Stack Annie' and they had come to warn us about her with our prisoners.[4]

A local police warning must have gone out at sometime, however, for in Calne there was a genuine alert. Mrs Mary Grafton worked in the Calne post office as a counter clerk. She recalled:

I can remember coming on duty one winter morning to find that there were several guns on the first floor landing of the post office. In those days the office was on the Strand opposite the Lansdowne Hotel. The three-storey building was demolished in the 1950s.

Everything that morning seemed to be shrouded in mystery but we all gathered that some emergency had arisen or was about to happen. We were a very young female staff so it was a good job we weren't called on to operate the firearms! Later we heard about the mass break-out.[5]

At Kensington Palace Gardens, Lieutenant-Colonel Scotland and his teams of interrogators could at last try and get to the bottom of the mystery. Had there been a genuine plan for the entire camp to break out with outside help from Germany? Were there agents loose who had made contact with the prisoners at Devizes and other camps, orchestrating mayhem?

The majority of those taken to the London Cage were soon found to know virtually nothing about the alleged plot. The questioning of the thirty-two prisoners lasted only five days and was undertaken in an efficient and detailed manner between 16 and 20 December. Scotland's opening paragraph of his report read:

> It has been quite clearly shown that all outside liaison to aid the plan for a mass escape from DEVIZES, i.e. British agents, American agents, secret wireless stations, airborne and seaborne support from GERMANY and collaboration with other PW Camps in SW ENGLAND as mentioned in previous reports, are fiction. They were all the invention of WUNDERLICH who wanted to increase the potential of the plot and his own importance in the eyes of his comrades who were participating.[6]

Of the thirty-two detained in London, Scotland wrote off twenty-five who either had no idea of Storch's plans or who had only heard vague rumours. Of the remaining seven, several had some form of superficial involvement, leaving only Storch and Wunderlich as the main conspirators. Scotland did uncover, however, a degree of cunning by the two ringleaders and a major problem with the general security within the camp as a whole.

Storch had been uncovered by an American Intelligence Officer on attachment to the camp from XVIII Airborne Corps. There were at least two other such officers. Two of them, Frank M. Brandstetter from New York and Joseph L. Hoelzl from Louisville, Kentucky, were awarded the American Bronze Star for their work in initially trying to get to the bottom of the plan. Unfortunately, with hindsight the truth of the whole affair is somewhat embarrassing. For although Storch was indeed persuaded to cooperate with the Americans and the British, at the same time he was planning a separate escape for 700 men. It appears that the bringing forward of the date for the break-out was, in fact, the result of Storch trying to put into motion his own plan, knowing what he did while in contact with the authorities. All of this spilled out in London.

Having been questioned by the Americans, Storch continued the façade of working under Wunderlich. The truth was that he now took over the planning of a much smaller break-out. In London Storch declared that he would not have 'trusted Wunderlich's ability to lead and carry out the plot' although his own abilities must also have been in question. Describing Storch's new role, the PWIS(H) report stated:

> STORCH continued to act a double role right up to the time of the arrest on 14 Dec of the 32 persons involved. On the one hand he informed almost daily on the major developments in the escape plan, on the other hand he did in fact formulate a reasonably logical escape plan embracing some 6/700 fellow PWs which might eventually have been put into effect, with or without his genuine participation, once the planning stage had been completed. He went as far as to contemplate involving an officer who would take over the leadership from him and relieve him of the responsibility, though in fact he had no chance to put this into effect. The officer in question was the chief German Medical Officer at DEVIZES, an O/Stabsarzt in Airforce uniform believed to be O/Stabsarzt GLEITZMANN who on the 7 Dec 44 was transferred from DEVIZES to No. 194 PW Camp.[7]

PWIS(H) described Storch as 'a congenital liar'. Initially, on questioning, he had claimed that the reason behind his own planned escape was to destroy, once back in Germany, some incriminating papers that linked him to the Communist Party back in the early Thirties. To Colonel Scotland and PWIS(H) this was pure nonsense, although such a line would undoubtedly have been used against him. Indeed, all PWIS(H) had to do was to let it be known in the camp that he had been a 'communist' and his very life would have been in danger.

On 13 December Storch, still at Devizes, was thoroughly questioned and it is likely that what he revealed led to the final round-up of all those implicated. Storch, it was discovered, had used Wunderlich as a cover to obtain some of the detailed information his own plan required, although this was woefully thin in the circumstances. His information came from four main sources: first, those who were slipping out of the camp to steal food and cigarettes from the American hospitals; second, those who had been on genuine working parties in the local area, including Le Marchant

Barracks; third, those who had been able to slip out during the previous month and thus had a more detailed knowledge of the surrounding countryside; and finally, those who were willing to pool their resources from other compounds. Using Wunderlich as a figurehead, Storch managed to obtain a fairly detailed idea of life outside the wire. PWIS(H) estimated that Storch had a reasonable idea of where his break-out men could obtain arms, food, vehicles and fuel. He also knew of at least two airfields nearby, RAF Yatesbury and RAF Upavon. But he went badly wrong, however, in believing the rumours about agents and a hidden arms cache – the latter based on Beier's finding of the detonators in November; he also believed that there was a large tank park nearby.

Most of the prisoners Storch planned to break out were housed in the A Compounds, A-1 to A-3, with another possible fifty or so from H Compound, normally used as overspill accommodation. Storch was able to persuade Wunderlich to visit all the A Compounds, having been given the necessary passes to do so by Corporal Hermann Bultmann who worked in the central camp office. (Such passes were used to allow work details access to different parts of the camp. Details were given to the central camp office and the relevant passes issued.) In H Compound Wunderlich had recruited an SS Unterscharführer, Fritz Hufnagel. Storch then took over the liaison with this prisoner and used him to recruit more manpower for the potential escape. In A-1 Compound Wunderlich had recruited another SS prisoner into the team, Rottenführer Heinz Brüling, but under interrogation, Storch had admitted that this man had not been the first choice. Previously it had been Goltz but on his detention after the November escape, he was no longer available.

On 13 December Storch, through Wunderlich, had organised a meeting in the camp medical centre during the morning sick parade. Still acting as a 'Chief of Staff' to Wunderlich as far as the other prisoners were concerned, Storch was to give orders to those in A-1 and A-2 Compounds. Part of the written agenda was, in fact, discovered during the arrests the following night. The Scotland report stated that Storch had demanded that, 'Each leader is to report to me the precise strength of each arm under his command, i.e. tank personnel, infantry, MT drivers, pilots and other flying personnel'.[8]

Back in London, Storch was again interrogated. He admitted he had dabbled with the local Communist Party before the war, but denied becoming a Party member. He then owned up to the fact that his real reason for trying to escape was that he felt homesick. He admitted to having used Wunderlich for his own personal ambitions. When asked why he had made so much up, especially the story of the arms cache, Storch declared:

> I was suspected by the American authorities of being the leader of the escapers. I was told that I would have to answer this charge and prepare my defence. On my own suggestion, to make up for this offence, I offered to do the American authorities a service to alleviate my punishment. As I already knew about BEIER's detonators, I told the Americans and they ordered me to find out further details.[9]

When asked again why he had cooperated with the Americans to such a degree, Storch admitted it was 'to alleviate my punishment . . . and I considered the chances of success as hopeless'. Later on, when asked why he had de facto taken on the leading role, he stated, 'this I did solely in order to find out the details of the plan, so as to pass them on to the American authorities'.

In turn, Wunderlich readily admitted under interrogation that he had made up a lot of the information. He stated to PWIS(H):

> I first met STORCH in the Detention Compound, but did not tell him anything about this matter. He said he had made plans for an escape, but had been given away a quarter of an hour beforehand.
>
> As regards the two agents, I have invented everything. GOLTZ, whom I told about this story, said it would just about be ideal. The story about the wireless apparatus I have also invented.
>
> Later I was released from detention and returned to A-3 Compound. STORCH also was placed in this compound some time afterwards. He asked me how I was getting on. I replied that one just had to carry on somehow. Next he asked me whether this story about two agents was true and I said it was. He wondered if they would be calling again and I replied that I thought they would.[10]

Wunderlich went on to recount how he and Storch then discussed how many prisoners could be persuaded to go with them and how the plan could be made to work. Wunderlich stated:

Six men should go through the wire to cut the telephone wires leading to the various sentry boxes; at the same time the guard should be disarmed but no shots to be fired; the six men should then open the gate. STORCH, with 200 men, would then at once proceed to occupy the Barracks [Le Marchant] and the American Hospitals and A-1 should start up simultaneously. They also were to disarm the guards and proceed towards the barracks.[11]

Soon after, Storch apparently persuaded Wunderlich to try and recruit further prisoners in H Compound, through the prisoner Fritz Hufnagel. By this time, however, the camp authorities were aware of what was going on, thanks to Storch's cooperation. Wunderlich stated that before he could get out of his compound to see the others he was spotted by Staff Sergeant Reis, the interpreter and number two to Captain Craig. Reis had been making his rounds on a bicycle at the time and, according to Wunderlich:

> . . . after a few yards I noticed that the interpreter was following me. So I went to the CRS [Casualty Reception Station, or medical hut], urinated, and returned. I went at once to see STORCH and he said that we should not in future be seen together. Then he declared the 'Stand To'. I suggested that he might want to alter the password . . . he replied that I should tell all those concerned that the password would be KOLN. I told everyone. Finally he was going to see all the leaders at the CRS but that was no longer possible as BRÜLING was placed under detention and later on I was also put under arrest.[12]

So ended the rather ridiculous 'Devizes Plot'. PWIS(H) went on to make a number of far-reaching recommendations in light of what had transpired. Scotland and his men concluded that, had Storch not 'turned traitor', then a serious situation might have developed. Storch's own plan, they surmised, 'could have been put into operation as an armed uprising'. PWIS(H) went on:

> The arrest without warning on 14 Dec of 28 suspected PW followed later by four others, had an immense moral effect on the thousands of PW remaining in the camp. The importance of making PW en masse feel the weight of our control when they attempt to break the peace cannot be over estimated. The eye-witness experience of one of the interrogators at the time, and the testimony of the four PW who arrived later, show that the whole camp was profoundly impressed by the arrest, the security

measures taken and the word of warning given afterwards by the camp Commandant.

The majority of the PW interrogated on this case gave the impression directly and indirectly that they had nothing else but escape to think about for 24 hrs a day as they were not given, in the majority of cases, any opportunity to occupy their mind or body in some constructive occupation.[13]

How right they were. Had immediate action been taken on the production of the PWIS(H) report, throughout all the camps in Britain, innocent men would not have been murdered later on.

Indeed, it would appear that the camp authorities both in Devizes and elsewhere were having a tough time of it. In 1941 there had been an extraordinary affair concerning a U-Boat captain, Kapitanleutnant Rahmlow. He and his crew in U-570 had been caught on the surface, quite by chance, by a patrolling aircraft which bombed the submarine. Rahmlow had surrendered his boat which was later boarded and taken to Barrow-in-Furness. Rahmlow was separated from his crew, quite rightly, and some of his officers ended up at Grisedale Camp. Within days, three of the U-570's officers were brought before a German 'kangaroo court' and tried for treason, for having allowed their boat to fall into enemy hands. The Third Officer, Oberleutnant Bergmann, was found 'guilty' and immediately shunned by the camp inmates. He was so distraught that he asked permission to commit suicide but this was refused. Instead, he was ordered to escape, go to Barrow-in-Furness and sink U-570 in the dock. Bergmann succeeded in getting through the wire but was challenged by one of the guard. Refusing to stop, he was shot and killed. There were also disturbances at Penkridge Camp and the officers' camp at Island Farm, Bridgend. Perhaps the most worrying of all, however, occurred at Doonfoot Camp in Ayrshire where ninety-seven Italian non-cooperators managed to break out through a tunnel. Within a week they were all rounded up again, but it was another illustration of the troubles encountered by the British authorities; it all pointed to a serious problem with the security arrangements.

This problem had been recognised at Devizes by the prisoners themselves. Many of their guards were older men from the Pioneer

Corps, most of whom were medically unfit for active combat service. But the truth was probably even worse. At the time, British Forces were suffering an acute shortage in basic infantry manpower, especially after the high casualties suffered in Normandy. As late as 22 December 1944, the War Office announced its intention to call up a further 250,000 men to fill the shortfall, and at the same time agreed to allow the ATS to serve overseas for the first time.[14]

Even the daily newspapers were picking up on the problems. Quite by chance a *Daily Express* reporter, one Vivienne Batchelor, appeared in Devizes the day after the round-up of the prisoners. She had heard that there had been a major disturbance in the camp. She visited Dick Hurn in his office, but he showed her the door immediately. The reporter then moved off down the road and sat having a cup of tea with some off-duty guards who obviously told her a very over-dramatised account of the events. On 18 December, as the London Cage began to get at the truth, her story was run on the front page of the *Daily Express*.[15] Relating much of the original stories told by Storch and Wunderlich as fact, it was never corrected after the war. Consequently, the story today, as expounded by many a writer and sadly in Scotland's own work, has more likeness to a good fiction novel than anything else.

The story persisted, however. An American Forces' newspaper one year later published the fact that Frank Brandstetter and Joseph Hoelzl had both been awarded the Bronze Star for their work in breaking the plot. In an odd mixture of fact and fiction, the paper wrote:

About 7,500 German prisoners were to fight their way out of Devizes Prison, 100 miles west of London. They were to seize the prison arsenal, establish road blocks, cut communications, storm two nearby hospitals for supplies and transportation and then launch a lightning effort to capture three airfields and 2,000 Sherman tanks of the British 11th Armd. Div. which were nearby.

The first plane seized was to fly direct to Hitler with first-hand news of the offensive and to give the signal for Nazi reinforcements, standing by on Heligoland, off the coast of Germany, to embark in assault boats and midget submarines.

Within four hours of their prison break the German PWs planned to liberate all Army prisoners in camps within a 60-mile radius of London.

After securing airfields and tanks the prisoners were to assault a nearby port, thus facilitating the landing of seaborne reinforcements.[16]

All of this was arrant nonsense, although the paper also 'described' in detail what the plan was in Devizes, including the correct passwords. Finally, the reporter stated that Storch's Order of the Day had come from Hitler himself, which was clearly not true, although the text quoted was accurate. Unfortunately, to this day, some respected authors persist in claiming that this was the true story of the Devizes Plot. It was not.

Back home, a more immediate remedy to the guard problem was the use of Polish troops who were not needed by the active divisions in France and Italy. Many of these men were themselves graded far below standard. None the less, ten Polish Guard Companies (PGCs) were formed and deployed in an effort to alleviate the problem of guard shortages. Devizes was no exception. On 19 December Colonel Upton and his officers were informed that No. 5 Polish Guard Company would be formed and sent to Camp 23, replacing the Pioneer Corps men. The deployment of Polish guards had already taken place at other camps: No. 1 PGC had gone to 189 Camp at Durham Park in Cheshire on 20 November 1944, and No. 8 PGC to 184 Camp at Magor in Monmouthshire. Also on 19 December No. 6 PGC went to Camp 22 at Cumnock, Ayrshire, and the following day No. 7 PGC moved into Camp 21 at Comrie in Perthshire.[17]

No. 5 PGC was commanded by a most remarkable man, Captain Tomas Ogrodzinski, with Lieutenant Bronislaw Zbiegien as his second-in- command. Ogrodzinski had first served in the Czar's Army in Russia, before joining the Polish cavalry after the First World War. And he ruled his men with an iron will. His company was actually below strength on deployment on 19 December: it should have been 241 strong but could only muster 196. But within days, Ogrodzinski sacked two of his NCOs for being 'totally unsuited'.[18] Many of Ogrodzinski's subsequent requests for additional manpower, especially NCOs, survive today in the archives of the Polish Sikorski Institute in London.

There was very little love lost between the Poles and their new German charges. The Warsaw Uprising had finished in bloody defeat only three months previously. It was common knowledge that the Germans had used their foreign SS troops to crush the gallant efforts of the Polish Home Army while the Russian forward troops halted and waited. Some of those who survived the uprising and the prison camps afterwards, will always remember how the Soviet anti-aircraft gunners held their fire while the German bombers attacked Warsaw.

Many of the Polish guards could tell remarkable stories. Pawel (Paul) Bechler was just such a man. Now living in Roundway, Devizes, he arrived at No. 5 PGC in February 1945. Born in 1925, Pawel Bechler had still been at school when the Germans invaded in 1939. Taken into forced German labour in 1942 when aged only seventeen, he was employed in France on a variety of construction projects. In March 1944 he escaped and was hidden by the French Resistance until it was safe for him to cross the advancing Allied lines after the Normandy landings. He became a tank crewman with the Polish 1st Armoured Division, then fighting alongside the Canadians. Wounded in the late summer of 1944, Bechler spent some time in a hospital in Paris before rejoining his regiment in Holland. Soon after, he fell victim to pneumonia and this time was evacuated to Scotland. Being pronounced A-1 fit again at the end of January 1945, Bechler was asked if he would consider joining a Polish Guard Company. Having agreed, he duly arrived in Devizes on 10 February with nineteen other Polish reinforcements. Pawel Bechler still remembers the taxing daily routine he and the other Poles undertook to guard the prisoners:

Each morning at 08.00 hours the guard for the day would be inspected. We would then be on duty for twenty-four hours. Normally we would do several two-hour shifts – rotating between guarding, being on stand-by and sleeping. After the twenty-four hour duty, we would then be stood-down for a day to undertake normal duties, especially training. We lived in wooden barrack huts alongside the British soldiers and carried Sten guns – very unsafe weapons. We used to wear battledress with Polish shoulder titles and a red lanyard. Whenever we went to escort prisoners from the station to the camp, the Germans used to get very frightened when they saw us with our Polish flashes on our shoulders.

We used to enter the prisoners' barracks virtually every second night. This we did at different hours. We used to just pull back the prisoners' sheets and blankets to check they weren't dressed to try and escape. We were told that we must never allow things [escapes] to happen again. If we did find them dressed, we used to take them to the square and drill them until they could sleep soundly because they were so tired.

The camp had two wire fences and we used to patrol between the two. We couldn't shoot until a prisoner had started to cut his way through the second fence and then we had to give a warning. Then we also had guard dogs. They were horrible animals. They could climb the steps of the [guard] towers and would bark if they found you asleep up there.[19]

Pawel Bechler also used to escort prisoner working parties of upwards of fifty at a time to the hospitals opposite:

The prisoners didn't like me. They used to say, 'Don't go with that little bugger, he never lets you bring anything back'. I never did either. We were ordered to ensure they didn't take anything in case it was diseased with things like gangrene. I used to get them to empty their pockets. If they wouldn't, I used to threaten to shoot them. We always had to do what the officer said.[20]

On the night of 23 December 1944, just over a week after the round-up of the main escapers, another escape attempt was made by a *Luftwaffe* prisoner. The Poles had no hesitation in opening fire and Obergefrieter Hans Kohn was shot dead. The following February, a more serious attempt, involving eight *Luftwaffe* personnel, was made on the southern side of the camp by the canal. Their attempt was recorded in a terse note in the Salisbury Plain District War Diary thus:

On 27 Feb, 8 *Luftwaffe* PWs attempted to escape but escape was discovered. They disobeyed the guards' orders to halt and they opened fire, killing one and wounding three. One further PW sustained a slight wound from a stray bullet, whilst in his hut.[21]

The Adjutant, Dick Hurn, also remembers that night:

In the new year, we started to get some very bad prisoners as they [the authorities] probably thought we could cope! In February, Colonel Upton's wife had a bad accident and we had to have a new commandant, Colonel Ayers. Before he arrived with us, I was temporarily in charge. It happened that the new CO arrived on the night of the new break-out. We were having a small party in the Mess to welcome him when a message arrived saying that there was shooting up at the main camp. A sergeant then reported that there was one dead and four wounded.

I went up to my office in one of the wooden huts and decided to sit on the floor in the dark, just in case. Eventually I was able to ring the new colonel with information as to what was happening. The escapees had been caught climbing out of a tunnel in the [canal] bank. When I rang him again, he asked me what was going on. All he said was 'Good show, keep me informed', and then rang off! That was the only night I ever put my pistol on.

The dead prisoner had been hit very badly with a Bren gun by a Pole. We paraded the hundred worst prisoners past the body in the mortuary and explained to them that this is what would happen if they tried to escape. The prisoner wounded in his hut was hit in the behind.[22]

Pawel Bechler also remembers that night very clearly. Although not on guard duty that night, he was obviously called out:

The prisoners were seen trying to get through the first wire fence and were shot. I was told that they [the guards] had to cut a hole in the second fence and push them [the prisoners] through so that they didn't get into trouble.[23]

The prisoner who died that night was Gerhard Lehmann, an Unteroffizier in the *Luftwaffe*. He was twenty-two years old.

Despite the continuing failure of the prisoners to escape from Devizes, attempts were still made, usually by tunnelling, especially while the war was still being fought in Europe. At the same time, a degree of fear caused by the arrival of a number of 'Black' prisoners swept through the camp. Dick Hurn again:

We had one or two so-called suicides, where we found prisoners hanging in the latrines. We would try to find out what had happened but it was always very difficult. We also found at least one tunnel as I recall, going out under the wire.[24]

'Charlie' May, the camp's odd-job man was one of those who found a tunnel in 1945. He also witnessed what happened when he found it:

In some of the huts they had secret trapdoors. I found a trapdoor and knew they would try to escape. They used to line the sides of the tunnel with the sacking they used to collect to make slippers, so it wouldn't collapse. One morning all the Germans started singing their marching songs and a prisoner whispered that there was an escape on. He even showed me the dug earth. Then the tunnel collapsed. Several other prisoners grabbed him and dragged him off to the toilets. I was told they had held his head under the water until he drowned. Then they hung him up.[25]

In many of the German camps that bleak winter, the 'Black' prisoners were meting out harsh, even murderous, treatment to any men thought to have transgressed the Nazi codes or shown any form of cooperation with the camp authorities. A new phenomenon developed – the 'Rollkommando' – a self-imposed and self-elected internal prisoner police force. Should a prisoner be reported to this mob, then he was brought before the 'Ehrenrat' and tried. Unfortunately for one former Devizes prisoner, caught up in the escape plans of that December, the experience was to end in murder and the eventual execution of five German prisoners of war.

CHAPTER NINE

Into the Lions' Den

The vengeful passions are uppermost in the hour of Victory.
Captain Sir Basil Liddell Hart[1]

On 24 December 1944 the Headquarters Salisbury Plain and Dorset District issued an order classified 'Secret and Immediate'. This order was sent throughout the area with copies also going to the Chief Constable in Devizes, the Headquarters US Southern District, and the Headquarters of the 8th US Armored Division in Tidworth. The order read:

> In light of possible coordinated escapes from PW Camps during the Xmas period, the following precautions will be put into force during the period Sunday, 24 Dec 44 to Tuesday, 26 Dec 44, both dates inclusive:
>
> (a) Guards will be increased to a maximum.
> (b) Inlying pickets to be detailed.
> (c) Sentries will be instructed to challenge once and shoot to kill.
> (d) PW will be warned accordingly.[2]

This order reflected the continuing unease that gripped the POW camp authorities up and down the country. In those camps with a known unruly element, the scare was even more pronounced. Consequently, the Christmas of 1944 was a bleak one. The German Ardennes offensive was continuing to push back the American forces and the Germans as yet, due primarily to bad weather, had not been checked. With open access to newspapers and radio, most German prisoners were able to follow roughly what was happening. The attack could hardly have come at a better time. With V2s still falling and the German armies once again victorious, the tide of war appeared to be changing.

In Camp 21, just outside the small Perthshire village of Comrie, in Tayside, there were celebrations. Despite the severity of the guard regime imposed by No. 7 PGC, who were all too willing to shoot first and then ask questions, as well as the prisoners' own hardliners from the SS and other ardent supporters of National Socialism, the prisoners' morale was sky-high.

Comrie itself had had a long, direct association with Scottish history. Known as 'Shaky Town' owing to its proximity to the Highland Boundary fault-line, Comrie had become a popular town in Victorian times on account of its 'tryst' (cattle market), which was attended by buyers and sellers from all over the Highlands. Nestling as it does among the foothills of the Highlands, Comrie would have been judged to be an ideal location for a prison camp. In the winter, the weather was very bleak and this, combined with the terrain of hill and 'strath' (valley), made escape on foot a very strenuous enterprise, to say the least.

Since the early days of the war, the residents of Comrie had grown used to the presence of German prisoners. They had watched with curious detachment, back in May 1941, as pioneers from 249 (Alien) Company, Pioneer Corps, had constructed a purpose-built POW camp just outside the town at Cultybraggen. Most of those involved in the work at the time were former German refugees. One of them, Mr Brook, now happily settled in Britain, can look back on those early days:

> 249 Company, Pioneer Corps, consisted of approximately 95 per cent of volunteers of German and Austrian Jewish refugees. We were at Comrie from about May to late September or early October 1941. To the best of my memory, we laid the foundations of the camp and I remember distinctly the erection of the barbed wire fencing. Our relations with the local inhabitants of course were excellent and on a recent visit to Comrie, I found that many people remembered us with affection.[3]

Nora Hamilton, interviewed by the BBC some fourteen years ago, recalled:

> When we heard that the first prisoners were coming, we all went down to see them arriving, which was a great event in the village, because the war hadn't really hit us very much, apart from the boys going away.
>
> The Italians came first and they were all playing guitars and having a wonderful time, skipping and jumping, going up Dalgenross. Then the next lot were the Germans. I think they were the SS. They were very soldier-like people, very firmly guarded.[4]

Jenny MacGregor also remembered the Germans being marched up to the camp:

> I do remember them always arriving on a Sunday, somewhere about midday. They were marched through the village and they sang their heads off. The Germans were very arrogant when they marched up. I'm quite sure their songs were running down the British.[5]

Lawrence McCulloch was a young Comrie schoolboy when the first prisoners arrived at Comrie:

> At first it was a transit camp and it was the 'Blue Caps' who brought the POWs to the camp by train and the camp guards who escorted them out to the camps. Then the Afrika Korps and full band arrived and there they stayed. There was a high security unit which held SS and German army officers. They used to hold their own courts and dealt out punishments.
>
> There was an SS German who posed as a Pole and was on guard duty when a fellow from his own SS unit went to talk to him and was shot. The Polish Army dealt with him so I was told.[6]

There had been several escape attempts prior to December 1944, but those who did get past the wire were soon rounded up again. But Camp 21 differed from other camps in the severity of the Nazi rule inside the wire. By the end of 1944 Comrie Camp was well known for this, and was often referred to as the 'Black Camp of the North'.

At this time, there had been no deliberate policy of segregation into specific camps, although detailed screening of individuals was called for again but in a more thorough manner. Henry Faulk, who became one of the leading exponents in the final prisoner Re-education Programmes, wrote:

> There never at any time existed among the POW camps of Great Britain a 'White' or a 'Black' camp, in the sense that all the inmates of the one were untainted by Nazi attitudes, whilst all the inmates of the other were steeped in Nazi ideology. Every camp consisted of a small 'white' element and a small 'black' element, rarely making up more than 20% of the camp total between them, and some 80% of 'Greys', men in whom National Socialism was simply the expression of group conformity. Nonetheless both prisoners and PWD spoke of 'White', 'Grey' and 'Black' camps. The reference was to the 'tone' of the camps, the awareness of

preponderant attitudes to which the mass conformed and which emanated from the small active element.[7]

Werner Busse was a German SS prisoner who spent the first three months of his captivity in Comrie Camp, before being shipped out to a camp in America. Busse had volunteered for the SS when only sixteen and a half years old. Posted to the 10th SS Panzer Division in France, at that time re-forming after the surrender in Tunisia, he was trained as a tank crewman. On 10 July 1944 the 10th SS was heavily engaged in the battle for Hill 112. Busse was then a tank commander and although wounded, he survived and was captured. After a short spell at a camp near London, Busse was sent north to Comrie where he arrived at the beginning of August. Of the camp in general, he had this to say:

[Camp 21] was a 'hard camp'. Among others of the German Armed Forces there were mostly members of the German elite . . . members of the Waffen-SS. The discipline was very strong and our morale very high. I myself was quartered in A Compound, hut No. 1. At first we had British personnel as guards which were later changed to Polish guards. They were very abusive to us and did not like us at all. Should one of us try to retrieve a football and crossed the so-called 'trip wire' they would shoot on sight. [This is] what I have seen personally.

The administration was as any other POW camp. We could send so many letters and postcards a month via the Red Cross in Switzerland. Our own discipline was still on the lines of the German forces and we still had a proud bearing. There was of course a minority at the camp which did not believe in the German victory any more. At that time there was no work done by the POWs. Otherwise we kept the Nissen hut spotlessly clean and there was a roll call every morning.

I remember one incident at the camp when a German NCO of the *Luftwaffe* was sentenced to death by the . . . court martial because he tried to influence other members of the camp to speak out against Hitler and the Nazi movement.[8]

Gunther Schran, having passed through Kempton Park in the hands of CSDIC also ended up in Comrie. He subsequently recalled:

We had three compounds, two for the Army and one for the Navy. The third compound was practically all submariners and they were all classified as 'C'.

[Our] treatment was actually quite good, the food was quite good. We were allowed to leave the camp but on word of honour, in groups of about 30 or 40, to go for a walk. Mind you only certain people. I am glad to say everyone kept his word and nobody absconded.

Christmas 1944 was just another morning, then of course we heard about the 'Battle of the Bulge' – Rundstedt's offensive and again people thought, 'well, perhaps old Adolf will still do it, he will still pull it off'. But of course that was a flash in the pan, as you know. While that was going on, Aachen had already fallen. They were already on the Rhine.[9]

To the outside world, Comrie appeared to be a model camp. As late as May 1944, before some of the prisoners from Normandy had arrived, the Red Cross had inspected the camp, as required under the Geneva Convention. In July the same year they published their findings thus:

On the 13th May, Dr J. Wirth visited Transit Camp No. 21 which had taken over the complete German compliment from Camp No. 24 as well as several hundred prisoners of war from the Afrika Korps fifteen days beforehand. Concerning the accommodation, sanitary arrangements and food, this is a good camp, but there are certain complaints concerning clothing (the African prisoners were not issued such items for over two weeks after their arrival) and . . . insufficient items to be found in the canteen.[10]

While the prisoners were being questioned in Devizes during late November and early December 1944, the authorities in Comrie faced their own problems. The influence of the few 'Black' prisoners was starting to tell to such a degree that the general daily camp routines were being turned upside down. In fact, so bad was the situation that CSDIC were called in to try to get to the bottom of the problem. What they found, and subsequently published, must have made chilling reading at the time.

Report M.I.19(a)/2278, marked TOP SECRET and published on 19 December 1944, was sent to the PW Directorate with the following short introductory note:

P.W.1
In view of the increase in escaping plots and nefarious activities in several camps of late, you may care to show D.P.W. encl. 1A & B.

If there are any further investigations you would like us to make, please let us know.[11]

Inside was a frightening tale of terror at Comrie Camp. CSDIC had obtained the information by eavesdropping on two German officers who had recently been removed from the camp. These two were Major Zapp, formerly of the 16th Sicherungs ('Line of Communication') Regiment and Wachsmuth, the former Commandant of the German Military Hospital in Brussels. Both had been captured early in September when Brussels had fallen to the British Guards Armoured Division. They were first overheard on 14 December and it appears that their discussion was so disturbing that a British officer from CSDIC subsequently interviewed the two together the following day. The combined reports have survived in the Public Record Office at Kew.

Major Zapp had gone through the normal prisoner chain before arriving at Comrie in October 1944. He stated:

At COMRIE there were two sections for officers and two or three for other ranks. [Compounds] B and C were the officers' sections. There were about 1,000 officers in each . . . they were mixed together indiscriminately, just as they were taken prisoner – Navy, SS, paratroops, railway operating troops, TODT Labour Organisation, up to the rank of 'Oberst'. In this camp, the SS and paratroops had organised a regular system of spying on the other officers, which became a real terror. I was in [compound] C. In B it was far worse, there was a sort of vehmic organisation, that is secret police with executive powers. For instance, if they recognised a man who had made an anti-Nazi remark, then they pounced on him in the night. It was organised terrorism.

In [compound] C it was exactly the same and there was an SS-Sturmbannführer GOECKEL, who was in hut No. 1, who was, one might say, in control of the spying. He had spies under him in the other huts.[12]

One of Zapp's main complaints was the idea that the British would establish a camp – POW Camp 13 – solely for anti-Nazi prisoners. This plan had filtered through to many of the SS prisoners who threatened to send the names of any men who volunteered for the new camp to Germany, so that their families could be dealt with under the laws of 'hereditary guilt'. The previous day, Zapp had described to Wachsmuth his worries:

They had their confidential men in all the hutments and had compiled lists. Those lists were to be smuggled into Germany with exchange PWs. As soon as it was known that so many of us were to go to a special camp, they tried, with the assistance of the German batmen, to compile lists of officers who were being considered for this Camp 13. The English had picked about 200. An 'Unteroffizier' who worked in an English office is said to have got this list through to Obersturmbannführer GOECKEL by means of wounded who were exchanged – a works foreman from the TODT organisation was there . . . he had a wooden leg and they intended concealing the list in it. Of course a lot of officers were now scared stiff . . . that the SD [Sicherheit Dienst, Security Services] in Germany would get this list . . . and warn the censorship to look out for who's in Camp 13. An order was issued a little while ago that any PW . . . collaborating with the enemy shall pay for this with the lives of all his family and with his entire fortune.[13]

In the same recorded conversation, Zapp went on to talk about the Comrie Camp Lagerführer, Prince Urach, who had been instrumental in drawing up the list of all those who wanted to transfer to Camp 13. Zapp confided to Colonel Wachsmuth:

He's scared stiff as he himself has a lot of relatives who were arrested in connection with the 20th July [the Hitler bomb plot]. He was terrified that something would leak out and that others from the camp would denounce him by means of letters to Germany, saying he had advocated those ideas with the Camp Commandant; then he might be identified with the 20th July Putsch and his wife liquidated as a result.

Obersturmbannführer GOECKEL is a frightful fellow; he was the terror of the whole hut. He was an instructor at the 'Junker' school at TOLZ – that says enough . . . and he always made notes, about every individual there.[14]

On 20 December 1944 the 7th Polish Guard Company took station for the first time. With so many SS and Paratroopers in the camp, relations between the guards and prisoners did not even get off the ground. Albert Mai, a prisoner at Comrie, recalled some of the difficulties they had with the Poles:

One day we were served bad liver out of tins and this was prepared in the kitchen. All the prisoners were affected by a dreadful attack of diarrhoea. The barracks were locked at 10 o'clock at night, if I remember rightly, after which we were given a bucket . . . but that wasn't enough – all buckets ran over [as] everybody suffered from this diarrhoea. We had to use the toilet; it was late in the evening and night, and it was dark. When the Poles in the watch-towers became aware of this activity, they shot without any consideration, into the toilets.[15]

Georg Stephanides, another Comrie inmate, recalls:

Polish soldiers came as a [guard] around the camp and they'd shoot, shoot into the camp – because after 10 o'clock nobody could leave the barracks. Somebody from our barracks was in another barracks visiting somebody and it was five past ten and he got shot through the neck.[16]

Indeed, so bad did the situation become between the Poles and the prisoners, that comment was made in the first report from No. 7 PGC, submitted on 13 January 1945 to the Polish Military authorities based in Scotland. The report stated that the guards must refrain from referring to the prisoners as 'German swine' since this caused them to start throwing stones at the guards who, in turn, would start shooting. This was bad for morale and showed the Polish troops up in a bad light.[17]

It was into this melting-pot of violence and intimidation that twenty-seven of the thirty-two prisoners from Devizes arrived between 10 and 11 o'clock on the morning of 22 December 1944. Among them were Wunderlich, Storch, Zühlsdorff, Goltz, Herzig, Bultmann and Brüling, all of whom had played a part in the big plan at Camp 23. Some of the others who went to Comrie had been interviewed but exonerated of any involvement with the Devizes plot. For their own safety, and to save them from suspicion, they, too, had to move camps. Although some of the 'Black' prisoners such as Zühlsdorff and Goltz might well have felt more at home in Comrie, there was one man for whom the transfer meant, quite literally, death. This man was Feldwebel Wolfgang Rosterg.

Wolfgang 'Bint' Rosterg was born into a reasonably wealthy family in 1914. Rosterg's father had been a manager in the large German industrial chemicals conglomerate of IG Farben, and Wolfgang had visited the United Kingdom in the early thirties to learn more about the chemical business. Rosterg was very much imbued with the Nazi ideals that had brought Hitler to power, according to some of those he came across in England. But by 1944, however, Rosterg had lost his Nazi beliefs. In Devizes he was known by all, staff and prisoners alike, as an anti-Nazi. It was Rosterg who stood beside Jim Gaiger, the camp Clerk of Works, to warn the new prisoners of the futility both of escape and of the continued belief in National Socialism. Dick Hurn said of Rosterg and his immediate boss, Jim Gaiger:

> [Rosterg] had nothing to do with those sent north, in fact he had very little to do with the prisoners themselves. He was Jim Gaiger's interpreter and Jim was the DCRE's [District Commander Royal Engineers] man. Jim was in charge of the everyday maintenance of the camp. He worked with and around us all day, every day and everyone liked him. He was first class at his job. Joe, his brother, I think was in the Queen's Regiment and he had another brother in the CMP.[18]

In an interview for the BBC, Jim Gaiger had this to say of Rosterg:

> I knew him well enough for about a month . . . very thick, pebbled glasses, thirteen stone possibly, around about thirty mark. He didn't appear to be a cheerful person . . . he was just an ordinary man. [He had a] slight sense of humour when he used to say, 'Don't believe the lying bastard, Mr Gaiger, he's telling you a pack of bloody lies'. He didn't seem the sort of bloke to me who would blow the gaff on anybody. Mind, I could be wrong about this but he didn't seem as if he would betray his own men, his own countrymen.
>
> If he was for Hitler I don't think he would have been as willing to be an interpreter as he was. He must have offered to do the job. And if you're a Nazi, then you would lie low, wouldn't you.[19]

Unfortunately, Wolfgang Rosterg did not lie low. The night after his arrival at Camp 21, on 23 December, he was dragged from his bed, brought before a hastily convened camp Ehrenrat in Hut 4 of B Compound and having been found 'guilty' was beaten to death in a manner that epitomised the hatred, anger and general savagery of the SS and other Nazis at the time.

Why Rosterg was detained in Comrie is difficult to understand. The London Cage report stated that he had had no knowledge of Storch's plans in Devizes and had not been involved. It was known, perhaps, that Rosterg was no supporter of the Nazis. He had, in fact, deserted in France. Apparently fluent in English, he was also a very keen reader of all the newspapers and other English publications he could get his hands on, including the POW camp paper, *Die Wochenpost*. This was written and produced under the auspices of the Political Warfare Executive of the Foreign Office. It was the only newspaper produced for the German prisoners during the war and was introduced only after detailed research into whether prisoners would accept it. First published in April 1941, it had to be cancelled in 1942 because of an invasion scare. Relaunched in November 1944, the eight-page paper contained worldwide political news and discussions, news from Germany, cultural and literary articles and general POW topics and letters. At the height of its production in 1947, circulation rose to some 110,000 copies. It finally ceased publication in 1948, when all repatriation of German and Italian POWs had finished.[20]

Undoubtedly, by December 1944, many German prisoners looked upon *Die Wochenpost*, also known colloquially by many prisoners as the *Lagerpost*, with some suspicions, often treating it with contempt in their belief that it was nothing more than British propaganda. It was, in fact, more than that, but it would have been difficult to persuade any of the SS prisoners that this was the case. On arrival in Camp 21, Rosterg reportedly asked to see the latest edition, thereby marking his own card with the Nazis and the 'spies' of Obersturmbannführer Goeckel. In turn, Goeckel and others would have heard from the likes of Wunderlich and Storch, Zühlsdorff and Goltz, that the Devizes plan had been betrayed. Certainly, Storch would not have dared to admit that he had cooperated with both the Americans and the British – and if another scapegoat could be found, all the better. Tragically for him, Rosterg fitted the bill admirably. Known for his anti-Nazi tendencies, known to have cooperated with the British authorities as an interpreter, known to have actively discouraged any escape from Devizes, and now demanding to see a copy of *Die Wochenpost*, he made himself a perfect target for the hard-liners.

Naval Obergefreiter Fritz Huebner was a prisoner in Hut 1 of B Compound at Comrie. In a statement made at the London Cage the following April, he recalled the newspaper incident:

On the morning of 22nd December, four POWs arrived from another camp and were put in my hut, No. 1. I recognised two of these men as

Zühlsdorff and Herzig. In the evening . . . there was a conversation. It was about the *Lagerpost*. Someone said that Rosterg had asked for the *Lagerpost*. Someone then said that if he had asked for [it] he could not be a national socialist. In reply Zühlsdorff said 'When I asked him if he was a national socialist Rosterg said "no, I certainly am not".' Zühlsdorff went on to say that Rosterg had said that he could speak seven languages and that he knew enough of the world not to believe in National Socialism. Zühlsdorff said that someone in the crowd had said to Rosterg 'Well, we will see about that'.[21]

Lieutenant Colonel Scotland wrote of Rosterg in his book:

. . . Rosterg committed the error of stirring up trouble among his own comrades by voicing criticisms of German operations in the Ardennes, the reports of which he read out to his hut-mates from the English newspapers.[22]

Albert Mai, another Comrie prisoner, told the BBC:

There were only a few of us who had questioned Rosterg about his activities . . . As I remember it, he admitted to some of us that he had worked a lot as an agent and that he had betrayed German 'ATS' girls, who worked as radio-telephone operators, to French partisans. He walked at first a free man after this . . . He really betrayed himself, gave himself away in saying that he was not one of us so-called Nazis . . . only then some of the others took notice of him and asked themselves, 'What sort of man is this fellow, who speaks so ill of us and calls us Nazi-swine? We must find out, not all is in order.' There were shouts of Nazi-swine and then the so-called 'raiding commando' [Rollkommando] really took notice of this fellow.

I believe that the English have to carry a lot of the blame themselves . . . It is my opinion that he was forced upon us intentionally in order to spy, listen and report . . . I can tell you this clearly now with hindsight – one should never throw anybody into the lions' den when the lions are irritated and worked up.[23]

Rosterg's fate was sealed. He was earmarked from the very beginning as a traitor who must die. Vengeance was the motive: vengeance for being captured, vengeance for not being able to continue the fight in the Ardennes, vengeance against what was seen as the betrayal of the Führer and of the honour of Germany. At last, a situation had arisen where all of them could show the world what they were really made of. Traitors must die and they must die by the rope.

CHAPTER TEN

Murder Most Foul

The basic aim of a nation at war in
establishing an image of the enemy is to
distinguish as sharply as possible
the act of killing from the act of murder
by making the former into one
deserving all honour and praise.

J Glenn Grey (1970)[1]

The true story of Rosterg's murder is appalling. He was beaten to
death and then strung up like a piece of meat in the latrines of B
Compound. The British authorities and their Polish guards must
have been horrified at what they discovered on the morning of 23
December 1944. But they cannot have been all that surprised. Only
three days before there had been a similar death in the camp: Major
Willi Thorn had been found hanging. His death was put down to
suicide, despite the circumstances being described as 'suspicious'.[2]

Yet the truth behind Rosterg's murder poses a problem for
historians in the shape of Oberfahnrich Erich Pallme Koenig.
Described by many as the son of a Vienna professor, in seven months
of active service Pallme Koenig had risen to the rank of Oberfahnrich
('Officer Cadet'). This rank was held by men in the ranks who
wanted to become officers, and was a probationary rank prior to
commission. Several authors have stated that it was Pallme Koenig
who had set up an escape committee and organised the Devizes
escape plan. The official records show that this is not the case.
Indeed, Pallme Koenig is not even mentioned in the official
documents that have survived, until Rosterg's murder in Comrie. His
name is not on the list of thirty-two prisoners taken to London for
questioning by Colonel Scotland and PWIS(H), nor is he mentioned
in the interrogation reports from Storch, Wunderlich or any of the
others who were questioned. Nor is there any reference to Pallme

Koenig ever having been at Devizes in the 'Summary of Evidence' produced for the deputy Judge Advocate General at the trial for Rosterg's murder. Even contemporary newspaper reports, some of which gave verbatim accounts of what was said, do not mention him at Devizes. Thus, the surviving evidence indicates that Oberfahnrich Pallme Koenig only entered the story at Comrie, not Devizes. His entrance, however, was to prove a disastrous one, not only for himself but also for four of his fellow prisoners. For Pallme Koenig was obviously one of those young SS men who still needed to prove his loyalty after only seven months' active service, as so many others were doing throughout the German camps that winter. He was a classic 'Black', and was to prove it on the night of 22/23 December 1944. His actions, however loyal to the cause, were to cost him his life just over eleven months later.

Altogether twelve German prisoners were eventually accused of murdering Wolfgang Rosterg. From the Devizes contingent there were Zühlsdorff, Herzig, Goltz, Wunderlich and Brüling. The remainder – Mertens, Pallme Koenig, Bienek, Recksiek, Klein, Steffan and Jelinsky – all became involved at Comrie. Of the twelve, only eight eventually stood trial at the London Cage in July 1945, and of them only six were found guilty. On 6 October 1945, five of those six – Pallme Koenig, Zühlsdorff, Goltz, Mertens and Brüling – were hanged at Pentonville prison. They remain there to this day, buried anonymously in unconsecrated ground.

★ ★ ★

For Wolfgang Rosterg, that night in late December, so close to Christmas, must have been his worst nightmare come true. In front of a howling mob of SS and other Nazis, he was repeatedly questioned and beaten. Several previous authors have tried to describe what transpired that night but there is little evidence in official records. Those who eventually came forward as witnesses really only described what they saw after reveille the following morning, the 23rd. Fritz Heubner, who was resident in Hut 1 described what he saw between 6 and 7 o'clock that morning:

Next morning, [Oberfeldwebel] Klein . . . came into my hut and told

Zühlsdorff and Herzig to go to Hut 4. He had a piece of paper in his hands and called the names out. Klein, Herzig and Zühlsdorff then left the hut and I followed out of curiosity. We went into Hut 4. There were already rumours going round that someone had been beaten up and I wanted to see what was going on. It was between 6 a.m. and 7 a.m.

I saw Rosterg standing in front of the stove. Klein said to Zühlsdorff and Herzig, 'Is that the swine who arrived with you yesterday?' Each of them said 'Yes'. Rosterg's face was badly swollen, so as to be almost unrecognisable. He had a rope around his neck. There was a noose at one end round Rosterg's neck with the knot at the back. Pallme Koenig was holding the rope, one hand about four inches behind Rosterg's neck and the other holding the rope a bit further back. Pallme Koenig said, 'Every time you scream, swine, I'll tighten the rope'. Rosterg could only groan, it appeared to me, because the rope was too tight around his neck. Bienek stood in front of Rosterg and read out from a paper which he was holding in his hands. Bienek said that the paper had been found either on Rosterg or in his kit, I do not remember which. The effect of what Bienek read out was that Rosterg had given away bombing targets and had been responsible for the rounding up by French patriots of German ATS women . . . After each statement was read out by Bienek, Rosterg was supposed to answer, but could only groan.[3]

Herman Bultmann was another ex-Devizes prisoner who was summoned that morning to Hut 4. In his evidence, Bultmann stated:

Next morning, immediately after reveille a naval Prisoner of War came into my hut [Hut 2, B Compound] and told us to get dressed straightaway and to come with him. He did not give any reason . . . he only told those who had come from DEVIZES to go with him. About 7 men left with me, WUNDERLICH and GOLTZ were two of them. We all went into hut 4. There was already a crowd in the hut and others seemed to be arriving from other huts. ROSTERG was standing by his bed. One man was facing ROSTERG . . . his face was badly swollen, blood was coming from his left eye and his lips were also badly swollen. He had a rope round his neck. There was a noose round his neck and the rest of the rope was wound round . . . later on it became unwound and the rope hung down. It seemed to me that RECKSIEK was in charge, all the others seemed to look to him for orders. There was a large crowd standing round . . . I saw WUNDERLICH among the crowd, also PALLME KOENIG.[4]

Bultmann went on to describe how he too was accused of being a traitor, 'I was therefore under emotional strain'. He was asked by the hut leader, Steffan, whether he had been a member of the Hitler Youth to which he lied that he had. This was accepted while the remainder of the crowd watched the continued questioning and beating of Rosterg. Bultmann again:

> BIENEK was there, he had a paper in his hand. I think BIENEK said that it had been found in ROSTERG's jacket pocket . . . BIENEK was translating parts of the paper and reading them out. It appeared to be extracts from ROSTERG's record. While BIENEK was reading from the paper a yellow file was being handed round from hand to hand among the crowd. I saw this file. WUNDERLICH's name was written on the inside of the cover. There were other lists of names of PWs who had been at DEVIZES. Lots of men in the crowd were saying that those lists were lists of Nazis to be given to the British authorities . . . I know in fact that ROSTERG was an interpreter, a clerk and wore a band with the words 'Compound Sergeant' while he was at DEVIZES and that those lists were lists of men for such things as delousing squads . . . ROSTERG was being hit in the face by men with their fists. When WUNDERLICH saw his name on the file he started hitting ROSTERG in the chest and face with his fists repeatedly. He was then held back by others in the crowd.[5]

Grenadier Otto von Goll was another witness to the events in Hut 4 that morning. In his statement he claimed to have heard cries and moaning during the night, drowned out later on by loud singing. The following morning, after reveille, he went next door as soon as he was dressed:

> I saw Rosterg standing to the right of the main entrance near the first window. His face was swollen, hardly recognisable and full of blood. His tunic had blood spots on it, about halfway down the blouse. He had a rope around his neck, Pallme Koenig was holding the other end of the rope; Bienek, who at that time had a small goatee beard, was standing opposite Rosterg and reading from a document. It was written in English; I knew this because I looked at it. While Bienek was reading this document Pallme Koenig urged the men who were standing around to hit Rosterg.[6]

Other witnesses testified that it was not only fists used to hit Rosterg: iron bars were also used. Wachmeister Wilhelm Foertsch from Hut 3 stated:

On the morning of 23 Dec 44, several inmates of my hut came back to Hut No. 3, after they had washed themselves, and said there was a traitor in Hut No. 4 who had arrived yesterday with a group of men from Camp 23. I took my small kit and on the way to the ablution room went into Hut 4, in order to see what was going [on] there.

Hut 4 was packed with people. At the right of the lower entrance, between two beds, stood Feldwbl. ROSTERG. His left cheek was coloured a vivid red and considerably swollen. In front of him stood PALLME KOENIG . . . [he] asked ROSTERG some questions. As he did not answer right away . . . [he was hit] in the face with an iron bar. The iron bar, which [was] used for this purpose, was one of those which fixed the boards, holding our belongings, to the ceiling of the hut. Rosterg lifted his hand to his cheek. When I saw that I turned around and went outside again.[7]

Huebner also recalled the use of iron bars to hit Rosterg:

There were about 100 men standing round while the 'trial' was going on. Recksiek picked up an iron poker from the stove and hit Rosterg on the right cheek and temple. He did this each time Rosterg was supposed to answer. Goltz also hit Rosterg with an iron bar which was lying in front of the stove and had been used as a poker. This one was square, whereas the one used by Recksiek was round.[8]

The assault on Rosterg must have been going on for a number of hours before reveille at 6.30 a.m. that morning. To some of the prisoners it was too much, even for a traitor. Many who witnessed the events went on to state that eventually the compound leader, Oberfeldwebel Pirau, was called into the hut by the hut leader, Steffan. The latter then pushed his way through the howling crowd, demanding them to stop as they must take Rosterg to the compound office. Pirau demanded that the rope around Rosterg's neck be removed, which Pallme Koenig duly did. Pirau and Steffan then escorted Rosterg out of the hut, followed by Pallme Koenig and many others.

Unfortunately for Rosterg, both Pirau and Steffan appear to have had little sway with the likes of Pallme Koenig. Inside the compound office, the beatings continued as they attempted to persuade Rosterg to sign a confession and then hang himself to redeem his honour. Obergefreiter Rudolf Vollstaedt worked in the office as a clerk. He remembered the group with Rosterg entering the office that morning:

On the night of the 22/23rd December 1944 [I] slept in the compound office. I got up shortly before 8 o'clock because I was room orderly that day . . . Rosterg was brought into the office . . . Pirau, the leader of 'B' Compound, came in with Rosterg . . . I recognis[ed] Pallme Koenig and Steffan as having been in the office. Bultmann and Camp Leader Claas were also in the office. When Rosterg was brought in his face was covered with blood. I continued dressing and making my bed . . . After about five minutes everyone left the room. Pallme Koenig went with them and then came back about 15 seconds or so later. Pallme Koenig grabbed Rosterg by the blouse, accused him of treason and said that he had many thousand Germans on his conscience. He called him a traitor. Rosterg said 'No, I haven't done it', and somebody who stood on his left side said, 'What, you haven't done it?', and gave him some blows in the face with his clenched fist. Pallme Koenig then told Rosterg, 'If you had any honour at all you will go and hang yourself', and Rosterg said, 'No, I cannot do it'. Pallme Koenig then told Rosterg to get out. Just before Rosterg left the compound office somebody put a rope round his neck and he went out with it on . . . I remained behind in the office.[9]

Herman Bultmann went to the office as well. He was also, or so he claimed at the time, under suspicion. Bultmann stated:

Everyone in the office took part in questioning me about my record. Rosterg was standing but I think he had been knocked about too much to know what was going on. Pallme Koenig grabbed him by the blouse and yelled at him to stand to attention while he was being questioned. After this Bienek arrived. Someone, I don't know who, ordered him to read out the same documents that he had had in the hut . . . After Bienek read some of the document, Pallme Koenig hit Rosterg in the face with his fist for not standing to attention properly.[10]

Heubner had remained outside the office with many others while Pallme Koenig had tried to get Rosterg to admit his guilt. He recalled what happened next:

After about five minutes PALLME KOENIG came out and said, 'Keep quiet, he has signed a confession and you will have him soon'. ZÜHLSDORFF was standing just outside the door. [Pallme Koenig] said, 'And I am making you responsible on your honour as a soldier. You are an SS man and you know what you have to do'. ZÜHLSDORFF replied, 'Yes' [and] PALLME KOENIG went back into the office. We waited outside.

The next thing that happened was that the door opened and PALLME KOENIG pushed ROSTERG outside . . . PALLME KOENIG said, 'Well, here you are, here is the swine'. GOLTZ fell on ROSTERG and pulled him to the ground. When ROSTERG was on the ground GOLTZ knelt on him and pulled the rope. ROSTERG was on his back and GOLTZ was on his chest when he pulled the rope. ZÜHLSDORFF and HERZIG kicked ROSTERG all over the body repeatedly. MERTENS was there and also kicked ROSTERG with his boots and pushed him with his feet . . . GOLTZ was holding onto the rope while this kicking was taking place. This lasted a few minutes. I was standing beside ROSTERG's body level with his thigh. I was about 3 or 4 feet from the body. There were shouts from the crowd, 'Hang him up, hang him up', and they started to drag ROSTERG towards the lavatory.[11]

Bultmann had been ushered out of the compound office and escorted back to his hut, Hut 2. He was then almost immediately summoned back, as were all the others from Devizes. Outside the office he witnessed what happened next:

There was a crowd of about fifty men standing outside the office. Almost as soon as I arrived, the door of the compound office was opened and Pallme Koenig came out and said: 'This swine is going to hang himself and if he doesn't you bloody well know what you have to do'. Pallme Koenig said, [pointing] to me, 'And I want to see that this tall fellow here is a proper National Socialist and takes part in it'. Immediately after Pallme Koenig came [and] made this statement, Rosterg came out of the office. He was pushed rather than walked. He staggered out as if he had been pushed. As soon as he came out Rosterg began to squeal like a stuck pig and immediately Goltz sprang on him and dragged him to the ground by means of the rope which was now round his neck. While he was still on his feet the crowd started to hit him and he collapsed and lay on the ground where the crowd began kicking him. Goltz sat astride on him . . . pulled the rope tight – with one hand he pushed the noose tight and with the other pulled on the rope. While Goltz was pulling the rope tight Rosterg was still squealing . . . They kicked him all over his body and his head and face. Stamping their feet on him is what I mean rather than kicking . . . While [this] was still going on several people had got hold of the rope and started dragging him.

Gefreiter Wilhelm Schmidt, having had breakfast at about 7.30 a.m., was on his way to undertake a coal fatigue when he passed the compound office that morning. He joined the crowd that was gathering outside. After a while the door opened and out walked Camp Leader Claas and Pallme Koenig. Schmidt testified that:

> He [Pallme Koenig] said, 'You had better keep quiet so that the sentries will not hear'. He may have said instead of 'sentries', 'Poles'. The German words are somewhat similar and in any event the sentries are Poles. Pallme Koenig also said, 'I will hand him over to you soon'. Then there was quite an interval. Then the door was opened and Rosterg was pushed out with a rope around his neck.
>
> Rosterg screamed like a stuck pig. Someone knocked him down and the whole crowd set upon him. Zühlsdorff was one of them. Mertens was another. An SS Unterscharführer knelt on Rosterg's body and pulled the rope tight. Somebody, I don't know who it was, stamped his foot on Rosterg's face . . . Zühlsdorff and Mertens took hold of the rope and began to drag Rosterg towards the lavatory . . . The crowd by this time had grown much larger as men from other huts had joined them . . .
>
> The lavatory has two entrances. The one through which his body was dragged was the furthest from the pipe from which he was hung. I entered the lavatory through the other entrance nearest to the pipe. When I entered . . . Rosterg was still on the ground, almost underneath the pipe. The rope was already over the pipe and Mertens was on the other end of the rope pulling. It was too heavy for Mertens and some men began to lift Rosterg's body up. I believe one of them was Herzig but I am not 100% sure. A tall blonde man whom I am almost certain was Zühlsdorff bound the rope round the pipe and made it fast . . . When Rosterg's body was made fast he was hanging about a foot from the ground. I then went with Merfeld to the kitchen.[12]

Heubner was also present when Rosterg was dragged off to be strung up:

> GOLTZ, HERZIG and ZÜHLSDORFF took hold of the rope and dragged him along the ground. ROSTERG's body was on its side. I followed. I think it was about 45 yards from the compound office to the lavatory. At one point a stone path had to be crossed. It was higher than the surrounding ground and caused an interruption . . . There were several hundred POWs who all knew what was happening and formed a crowd between the compound office and the lavatory and ROSTERG was dragged through this crowd. I followed the body about 7 feet behind it. The entrance to the lavatory was narrow, only wide enough for two people to go in at a time. GOLTZ and ZÜHLSDORFF dragged him through the entrance. MERTENS and HERZIG followed behind ROSTERG's body into the lavatory. I went in and stood on the other side of the partition which

divides the lavatory in half. The partition was as high as the level of my chin . . . There were a number of other POWs in the lavatory so that it was quite full of men. GOLTZ and ZÜHLSDORFF put one end of the rope over the pipe and MERTENS pulled on the end. It seemed to be too heavy for MERTENS and he said, 'Hold him up'. HERZIG and ZÜHLSDORFF held ROSTERG's body up. GOLTZ made the knot round the pipe and ZÜHLSDORFF assisted him. As soon as the rope was tight they all ran away. ROSTERG hung with his toes about 6 inches from the ground. He appeared unconscious. I went back to my hut. All the crowd went back to their huts. It was very nearly time for roll-call at 8.30 a.m.[13]

Brüling continued to boast about his part in the murder for several weeks. SS Soldat Charles Lergenmuller claimed in a short statement:

I went to visit him [Brüling] in hut 2. We talked about a number of things including the death of Rosterg. He said that Rosterg had betrayed the escape attempt at Devizes and . . . 'that's why we killed him'. He then said he was present and took part in the killing. He said he knew Rosterg and that Rosterg had come with him from another camp.[14]

Albert Mai remained troubled by the Rosterg murder long after the war was over. He remained sceptical about Rosterg's intentions at Comrie but that did not excuse what eventually transpired. In his interview for the BBC he stated:

I don't know if Rosterg was already dead by the time he was taken to the wash-room; if I remember rightly, he was strangled with a rope and then suspended from the water pipes.

This ought never to have happened; it was wrong to have killed this fellow; I deplored it . . . it was not correct . . . But it was also not correct to manipulate such a person into the camp in order to probably spy, or sound us out, particularly since he wore the German uniform. In my opinion they should have given him a sound beating and then taken care that he was taken out of the camp.

It should never have happened; I say to myself again and again that they should have removed Rosterg from the camp.[15]

It was after the camp roll-call at about 8.30 in the morning, that Rosterg's body was discovered by the camp authorities. It must have been a very grim sight. One of the first British officers on the scene was the camp medical officer, a major in the Royal Army Medical

Corps. Already others were trying to revive Rosterg using artificial respiration. Initially the major thought Rosterg might still be alive, having detected possible signs of life. It soon became obvious, however, that he was dead.

Existing records do not show what the immediate reaction to Rosterg's murder was. Certainly the camp authorities would have notified both the War Office and the civil authorities. All reports state that the first investigations were carried out by the office of the Procurator Fiscal. The case being recognised as one of possible murder, the examination of the scene and the post-mortem on Rosterg would have been carried out by civilian authorities, perhaps even by Scotland Yard, although records in the Public Record Office make no mention of the case in the index and if any papers have survived, they would probably be subject to a 75-year closure order as is the norm.

There were also problems because the killing had taken place in Scotland. Under Scottish law at the time, convictions for murder could only be proved on the evidence of two independent witnesses. How were such witnesses to be found in a camp that was ruled internally by the terror of the 'Rollkommando'? From the very start, therefore, it was clear that the authorities would struggle to move their investigation along to a final conviction. They did it, though. It took them six months but they indicted twelve men, five of whom were eventually hanged.

CHAPTER ELEVEN

Bolting the Stable Door

It's easy to make a man confess the lies he
tells himself; it's far harder to make him
confess the truth.

Geoffrey Household[1]

Even before Rosterg met his grisly end, the War Office, and DPW in
particular, were growing concerned by the violence in the camps.
This, coupled with the increasing number of escape attempts
throughout the country, must have caused serious concern. The
Devizes saga also demonstrated that there was no coherent policy in
force, nor even planned, to deal with mass break-outs. Those local
plans that did exist, such as the use of the Home Guard at Devizes,
were wholly inadequate. Consequently, on 12 January 1945 the War
Office signalled all Commands that they were to consider planning
for the possibility of a successful mass break-out of prisoners in their
areas and to consider their reaction.

Scottish Command was quick off the mark, perhaps as a result of
the Comrie situation. They produced and issued a document entitled
'Scottish Command Operational Instruction No. 28'. The object of
the plan was two-fold: first, 'to reinforce PW Camp guards in the
event of a plan for a contemplated mass break-out being discovered',
and second, 'to recapture PWs after a mass break-out'. Scottish
Command's plan envisaged the use of mobile columns made up of
troops based locally, mainly to be provided by soldiers from the
Infantry Training Centres (ITCs) and Local Defence Companies, as
well as additional Polish and Norwegian troops who were based in
the area. Manpower was at a premium, however. Consequently, it
was also stipulated that no troops dedicated to reinforcing 21st Army
Group – then fighting under Montgomery in Europe – were to be
involved. The whole plan was based on the issue of three code words,
'ASH', 'ELM' and 'OAK'.[2] The first would be used to announce that a

disturbance was expected and that reinforcements should be prepared to be sent to the scene; the second that reinforcements should be sent at once; and the last that large-scale escapes were actually in progress. The level of command was that of Sub-District which, in the case of Comrie, was HQ Tayside. Although for Scottish Command the plans were drawn up and issued in January 1945, amendments were still being issued as late as the end of March. In Southern Command, plans were submitted much later, in fact not until April, with final amendments not being produced until the following July.[3] In both cases, the local constabularies were heavily involved and Southern Command even went as far to incorporate plans into its instructions to cover general riots by the local population!

Although both examples might seem to suggest that the authorities were 'bolting the stable-door' rather too late, the plans were nevertheless a necessity in order to quieten a growing unease among the general public about what was taking place in the prison camps. Awareness was high – especially after the Devizes Plot report in the daily newspapers. In fact, so great was the public unease that by February, just over six weeks after the Rosterg murder, questions were raised in the House of Commons. On 20 February no less than four MPs asked Sir James Grigg, the Minister for War, to make a statement about clashes in POW camps between Nazi and anti-Nazi elements, organised 'assaults, trials and secret hangings' and the formation of 'storm troops by Nazi prisoners . . . who frequently intimidate other German prisoners'.[4] The Minister for War replied:

> There has recently been one clash between Nazis and other German prisoners at a camp in Canning Town. Some of the latter had to be treated by the camp doctor, but none died or were admitted to hospital. At another camp there has been one case of violence which resulted in the death of a prisoner. At four other camps there have been isolated instances of assault by Nazis on non-Nazis . . . Considerable progress has been made in the last months in segregating ardent Nazis from the rest . . .[5]

Grigg was referring to an ongoing segregation of prisoners that had first been proposed as far back as the late summer of 1944. Initially, such segregation had become necessary when there had been an almost total refusal by German prisoners to work. It transpired that any who did were accused by the hardline prisoners of 'aiding the enemy' and often beaten. Consequently, a new department was created at PWD to oversee a detailed screening and segregation programme in order to get German prisoners to work. Those Nazis who refused, or who intimidated others into non-cooperation, could then be weeded out and segregated. For the British, such a programme was fundamental to maintain the enormous agricultural effort needed to feed the country; the worsening manpower shortages due to continuing war casualties made the situation even more difficult. After all, the Women's Land Army could only do so much.

Another bonus for the British was that their American ally agreed with the general concept, although the Americans were less concerned with the requirement for additional manpower for their own needs, but more with the 'democratisation' of the prisoners in order that when they were eventually released, they would return to a new Germany with a political understanding that could never again accommodate a National Socialist ideal or political viewpoint. Thus for the Americans, screening was necessary before re-education programmes could be started, to wean German prisoners off their Nazi indoctrination. (And it should not be forgotten that for many prisoners, they had known nothing else.) All concerned saw the screening task as a purely military one, to maintain discipline in the camps. With hindsight, some of those employed in the screening process could be seen as being somewhat over-zealous by today's standards. The idea of prisoner re-education had first been proposed at the Teheran Conference of the 'Big Three' back in November 1943, during which Churchill, Roosevelt and, to a lesser extent, Stalin, agreed that Germany after defeat should be demilitarised, de-Nazified and 'democratised'. In Britain, the War Cabinet first started thinking about such a programme in a memorandum dated 14 September 1944; this was followed up on 18 September by another that directed that PWE should have overall responsibility. Of course, re-education had to go hand-in-hand with the screening process. There was, after all, no point in trying to re-educate the known anti-Nazis or 'Whites'. Indeed, some suggested that these prisoners could be actively involved in the process and some duly were after VE Day in May 1945.

Some camp screeners were to become notorious: they were remembered by former prisoners for their harshness, even hatred; others, however, were fondly remembered for their understanding and even-handedness. At Devizes the camp Intelligence Officer's deputy, Reis, a German Jewish refugee, was one of the former. Matthew Barry Sullivan, a screener during the war, quotes two instances in his book *Thresholds of Peace* whereby he graded prisoners as 'C's – National Socialists – virtually straightaway:

At Devizes Hans Freiburger and his comrades all decided they would enter the screening hut with the 'Heil Hitler' and the Nazi salute. They were all immediately given C-plus . . . At the same camp Willi Wolf remembers a screener called Herr Reis who would shout out for those who considered themselves to be Czech, Austrian or Polish to step forward. 'It was shaming to see who did so to save their skins.' [Willi Wolf's] group also decided each to give the Hitler salute, at which Herr Reis would dismiss them immediately with a 'Nazi, Jawohl, 'raus!'[6]

For such a screening process to be efficient, every prisoner had to be seen individually. This required the mass recruitment of new interpreters. Notices went out throughout the country, to every Command and unit, for people who could speak German and were prepared to work with German prisoners. One such notice went up on the board of 249 (Alien) Company, Pioneer Corps. This was the company to which Herbert Sulzbach, the Jewish refugee from Frankfurt, now belonged. He immediately volunteered and was accepted, with instant promotion to sergeant. His first camp was Comrie.

Herbert Sulzbach personified the re-education programme right up to the closure of the last camps in 1948. The work that he undertook was to leave a lasting impression on many prisoners who came into daily contact with him. Sulzbach was, after all, a German. He would never renounce this. Instead he used it and his deep understanding of the German military ethos – he was, after all, a holder of the Iron Cross – to remould the minds of those so deeply imbued with the National Socialist doctrine. Sulzbach himself admitted that his first months in the job were not very pleasant. He had been forced to leave his country of birth because he was Jewish – and now he was going to work among the very people whose beliefs had made his life a misery for so many years. He wrote about his arrival at Comrie:

A murder was committed just before Christmas 1944 in Camp 21. The victim: a German Sergeant who had been posted to Comrie from another POW camp. The murderers: a group of fanatical Nazis, just some 4,000 German NCOs and other ranks at Comrie. The motive for murder: the fanatics had searched the Sergeant's kitbag, found his diary and saw remarks which indicated that the Sergeant no longer believed in Hitler.

In the early hours of the morning the unfortunate Sergeant was hanged. Later his body was found by the guards.

This was the atmosphere at Camp 21 when I arrived after Christmas 1944.[7]

Sulzbach had a number of tasks at Comrie. First and foremost, he was an interpreter, working directly for the Camp Commandant; two months after Sulzbach's arrival one Colonel Wilson, a former policeman, was appointed to this post. Sulzbach's second responsibility was to the Political Intelligence Department (PID) of the Political Warfare Executive (PWE) at the Foreign Office. PWE held the overall responsibility for the prisoner screening and, later, the re-education programme.

But Herbert Sulzbach also had a third task – he was to help track down the murderers of Wolfgang Rosterg. The initial questioning by the Scotland Yard team had got nowhere, which was hardly surprising since Comrie Camp was still held fast in the iron grip of the Nazi faction. Records show that escape attempts continued, one of which involved the digging of a 35-yard tunnel under the wire from A Compound. There had also been a sit-down strike by all the camp prisoners – all 3,095 of them – on 7 February 1945, after the Polish guards had shot and killed a prisoner. Hard measures were needed. The authorities wired off all the camp gates and declared the whole camp a detention centre, allowing the prisoners only bread and water for seven days. This broke the strike but not the Nazi grip.

Herbert Sulzbach found the work at Comrie very challenging. Not only did he have to overcome the prisoners' prejudices against the Jews, he also had to overcome his own fears of being so close to Nazis. In his interview at the Imperial War Museum, Sulzbach recorded some of those fears:

[Comrie was] a very fanatical and Nazi-minded camp with 4,000 privates and NCOs – Germans – fanatical ones. . . . When they marched to their football grounds, they sang the horrible Hitler marching songs . . . that was the atmosphere. They were ardent Nazis.[8]

Yet this did not deter Sulzbach, for he had found his true vocation at last, after so many months in the wilderness of the Pioneer Corps. In a letter to his mentor Captain Basil Liddell Hart dated 11 May 1945, Sulzbach wrote:

> My job is the most interesting I could imagine and I love it and I am as happy as a soldier can be; I volunteered to continue the job.
> What I saw here in these 4 months seems unbelievable and gave me right; 90% of the Germans are bad, very bad, fanatics and swines . . . daily new incidents and it is the intelligence job I was longing for; I enjoy the complete confidence of my Colonel and all Officers [and this is] what makes me happy.[9]

Colonel Archibald Kennedy Wilson CBE, KPM, the new Comrie Commandant, arrived at Camp 21 towards the end of March 1945. Born at Galston, Ayrshire, in 1890, he was educated at Bablake, a large private school in the Midlands, where he passed the exams for Liverpool University to read Veterinary Sciences. Sadly, a death in the family rendered this impossible and instead he joined the Cardiff Police in 1909.

In 1928 Archibald Wilson was promoted to the rank of Chief Constable at Carlisle, moving on to become the Chief Constable at Plymouth the following year. On 24 January 1932 Wilson's mettle was tested when he decided personally to lead a detachment of the Plymouth police detailed to go to the assistance of the county police in putting down a prison riot at Dartmoor. At the time, Wilson was dressed in plus fours and carrying an ashplant stick which the records show him as 'having no hesitation in using'.

Later that year Wilson moved to Liverpool, where he remained for four years. It was here that he first came to prominence, as a result of his handling of IRA activities in the city. In 1933 he was appointed to the Departmental Committee on Detective Work and Procedure by the Home Secretary personally. During this period of his career Wilson supported for the first time the idea of the police using radios and that they should be netted in to all police forces. He was an innovative man – while still in Plymouth he became the first Chief

Constable to introduce motorcycle patrols, buying two Sunbeams for the experiment. During his long police career, he was awarded the King's Police Medal and was made a Commander of the British Empire in 1937.

In 1938 Wilson was given control of the national Air Raid Precautions Organisation. He set about this onerous task with tremendous energy, creating the Air Raid Wardens Service of some 5,000 wardens, supported by some 12,250 firemen of the Auxiliary Fire Service. Throughout the war, this organisation proved its worth time after time during innumerable nights of bombing, a fitting testament to Colonel Wilson.

Forced to retire in March 1940 owing to failing eyesight and general ill-health caused by pressures of work, Wilson was later called up to DPW on the General Service List and was given command at Comrie, with the rank of full colonel. His police talents made him the ideal choice to oversee the detection of Rosterg's killers, as well as the general administration of the camp through the Nazi troubles. He wrote of his first impressions thus:

> I was posted to take command of this camp as Commandant on the 27th March 1945. I was at the time temporarily stationed in the North Highland District of Scottish Command.
>
> No intimation was given to me as to the situation at this camp but on making an inspection in company with the Colonel who was being replaced I found that the situation was far from satisfactory. As far as I could learn there had been escapes and that murder had been committed in the camp – that was, murder by prisoners of other prisoners.
>
> The prisoners in this camp were of the most truculent and intractable type – up to then quite unworkable. There was a large number of SS men – real shockers – a large proportion of men of the Africa Korps and also submarine men. There were no German officers other than 4 German doctors in the camp hospital. They maintained their truculent attitude but they looked somewhat thoughtful and they soon had cause to be.[10]

At the time of Colonel Wilson's arrival, Comrie camp was still packed to capacity as the full screening programme had yet to be fully initiated and there was insufficient alternative accommodation in which to place the newly segregated ardent Nazi prisoners. Apart from the 4,000 at Comrie, there were a further 500 prisoners at the

newly established satellite camp just up the road at Cowden (Camp
21A). Colonel Wilson deduced that his first task was to set out in
detail what he expected of everyone under his command – camp
authorities, guards and prisoners alike. He drew up detailed orders
for all, and sent some of the Polish guards away on dog-handling
courses. He also ordered a number of raised guard towers to be built
which, until then, had been lacking.

Escape attempts were still being made by the prisoners. On 9 April
a tunnel was found, its entrance concealed in a night latrine in B
Compound. Further searches the same day revealed the start of a
separate tunnel in a compound store-house. On 27 April a third
tunnel was found after a special search instigated by the
Commandant himself. Colonel Wilson wrote of this discovery:

> I had suggested to the [B Compound Leader] that he ought to get the
> men in his compound to improve its appearance by making beds and
> sowing and planting flowers.
>
> Between the partially disused QM storeroom – next to the wire – and
> the cookhouse was a large open square, full of potholes. I suggested that
> the prisoners might make up a circular mound of earth and plant it out
> with flowers I would get for them. As the soil had to be wheeled some
> considerable distance, this took some time. As the mound was building
> up, I took notice of it on my weekly inspections. And I also noticed the
> colour of the soil – dark brown. Then, on the occasion of an inspection a
> fortnight later, I noticed that the mound, now longer, was partially
> covered with soil of a yellowish-brown character. I had also noticed once
> when passing along the adjoining riverbank that underlying the topsoil
> there was a stratum of yellowish clay. I said nothing but was satisfied from
> this that a tunnel existed and I arranged a special search.[11]

By 4 o'clock in the afternoon nothing had been found. But Colonel
Wilson was still convinced that there was a tunnel so he ordered the
search party to start again. In the old QM's store Wilson himself noticed
an old round bin among a pile of discarded clothing and asked if it had
been searched. The search party cleared everything, even removing the
bin but still found nothing. In the end Colonel Wilson got down on to
his hands and knees for a closer inspection. He went on:

> I noticed on the cement floor a circle which was smaller than the outer
> rim of the big bin. I got down on my knees and was able to say, 'here is

the tunnel'. With the point of a bayonet we lifted out a circular block of concrete. This was not easy as the block fitted so closely. Underneath was a dark hole from the bottom of which a tunnel led out under the wire.[12]

Next, Colonel Wilson had to find the tunnellers. During the search the prisoners had been held on the recreation ground, but on discovering the tunnel, Wilson ordered them all to be lined up for inspection. He himself ordered every prisoner to present his hands, palms down. All those with yellowish earth under their finger-nails were put into detention. There was no more tunnelling.

Despite continuing unrest and the additional shootings of prisoners by the Poles, Colonel Wilson was able, at last, to start to unravel what had happened to Rosterg the previous December. He wrote:

Eventually I had time to get down properly to investigating the murder question. On this matter it will be understood that no details can be given but I employed certain Nazi psychological tricks. As soon as sufficient evidence was obtained against a suspect he was arrested in broad daylight in full view of all the prisoners. They saw the man marched off, disappear into the Detention Block – the only brick-built building in the camp – and that was the last they saw of him. He was removed in the middle of the night to the London Cage to await trial.[13]

Alongside Colonel Wilson and Herbert Sulzbach, now promoted to Staff Sergeant, was a young Army officer seconded from the Judge Advocate General's Department. John Wheatley (later the Right Honourable Lord Wheatley PC), had initially been trained for the Bar before being called up into the Royal Artillery. After attending OCTU at Catterick, he was commissioned and posted as a Troop Commander with 484 Battery of 119 Field Regiment. In 1944 he transferred to the JAG Department, where he was interviewed by the JAG himself, Brigadier Shapcott, universally known as 'Shappy', but not to his face. John Wheatley's first appointment was with the JAG Department of Northern Command based at York. Towards the end of 1944, Wheatley now a Captain, was posted again, this time to Edinburgh and Scottish Command. He soon found himself fully committed to the Comrie investigation. In his autobiography, he does not say much about what was to transpire, although he obviously played a significant part:

A case of suspected murder at a Prisoner of War camp . . . had been engaging the attention of the authorities for some time. A protracted dispute had taken place on whether the matter should be dealt with by the civil authorities or by the Army authorities. The Lord Advocate carried the day but he was unable to make any headway because of the lack of corroboration which the law of Scotland requires for a conviction, and there was only one witness forthcoming to speak of murder as opposed to suicide, which the death had been made to look like. The case fell back to the Army authorities and the JAG took over. Shappy sent word to my CO, Colonel Hallis . . . that he wanted me to take over the investigation. I did so, and with immense help from an interpreter who was seconded to me [Sulzbach] I picked up bit after bit of evidence which 'in cumulo' provided all that was required to involve a number of the deceased's co-prisoners of war in a murder charge. I sent all the statements which I had obtained, with relevant documents, to London where they were gratefully received.[14]

The investigations were made easier by the screening of prisoners and the removal of the most ardent Nazis from Comrie. These latter prisoners were sent off to Watten Camp, only completed the previous March. Camp 165 at Watten, in Caithness, the extreme north of Scotland, had been purpose-built in its remote location for one reason and one reason only: to house what were then termed 'CX' prisoners – those deemed to be extreme Nazis, some of them verging on the psychopathic. These were the really bad boys.

As always in such situations, reality takes over very quickly. In 1946 Watten had to give up its specialised role as large numbers of prisoners were returned from America. The camp was divided into two, with an 'A' Compound for German labour prisoners and the 'B' Compound retaining its CX category. The majority of the returning prisoners were put through the screening process, both to identify those who needed further re-education as well as to start the process of returning manpower to Germany where it was so desperately needed for rebuilding.

Outside Caithness, little is known today about the former POW Camp at Watten, since all the remains were bulldozed in the sixties. One man who does know about it, however, is Alexander Budge, a schoolteacher living in Wick. In 1990 he and his class produced an excellent study of the camp, contacting a number of former prisoners, including Charlie Hansel, a former *Luftwaffe* rear-gunner on Junkers Ju-52 transport aircraft. Captured in North Africa, Hansel had to endure the makeshift camps around Cap Bon in northern Tunisia, and later at Oran in Algeria before being shipped out to America. In 1946 he was returned to England. It appears that he failed his screening and instead of being repatriated he was transferred to Watten graded as a 'C'. He said of those days:

> We were interrogated every 6 months, I think. The interrogators were always Jewish, which from my point of view was wrong because obviously in view of what happened they had no time for Germans. First of all the interrogator went on about how Germany had thought they were going to win the war. Then he asked me who was responsible for all the German cities being in ruins. I told him that the people who dropped the bombs were. He started to call me very dirty names in German but I did not lose my cool. I just stood and took it. He started asking me about the concentration camps. I never knew such a thing existed although we had heard such things in America . . . the swearing continued, he wrote something by my name and then said 'dismissed'. He said [I would] remember this day for the rest of my life. That's how I ended up . . . in Watten.[15]

In Watten, those in the CX compound were very strictly controlled, often on a reduced diet. Charlie Hansel again:

> We got very little food, our ration was only half that of 'A' camp and it was cut further if someone tried to escape . . . occasionally we got out with the guards – very occasionally – and we stretched out the column as long as we could. So many sneaked into a turnip field and stole turnips.[16]

Doctor Hans-Dieter Sauter, a young medical student, also fell foul of the screeners as late as 1947. He had joined the Waffen-SS in 1941 and was commissioned in 1942. He saw active service in Russia where he was wounded three times, and then joined the 10th SS Panzer Division. Captured in Normandy, he spent his first two years as a prisoner in Canada, before being returned to England. In the summer of 1947 he was classified as still CX and dispatched to Watten. Of his screening he recently stated:

> Still today I do not know why I was classified 'C-plus' [CX]. Once an interrogator asked me: 'How many Jews did you kill?' I answered: 'Never

in my life have I seen a Jew, captivity excluded.' This was true but he yelled: 'You dirty German b—d' and similar names.

Then he asked me if I was married. I affirmed it, and he shouted: 'Do you want to see your wife again?' Again I affirmed it and he shouted: 'We shall hand your wife over to the Russians and put her in a brothel in the Caucasus mountains. There you can see her again.'

Then he threw me out. Apparently it was beyond the possibility of imagination of an interrogator that a lieutenant in the Waffen-SS had never seen a Jew.[17]

Camp 165 at Watten was used to house those prisoners transferred out of Comrie. This was done quickly, allowing Sir James Grigg, the Minister for War, to reply to a question in the House about further violence in German camps on 24 April 1945:

I referred to the incidents at Camp 21 in the answer I gave a number of Hon. Members on the 20th February. The suspected culprits in this case are being interrogated and so far four have been charged with the crime and will be brought to trial. A prisoner of war who was a witness in the case narrowly escaped being murdered and other witnesses were attacked and injured. Camp 21 has since been carefully screened and all known anti-Nazis removed. Ardent Nazis are segregated from other prisoners as soon as they are discovered and nearly a third of the German prisoners in our hands in this country have so far been removed from the rest as ardent Nazis.[18]

The four prisoners charged with the crime were Brüling, Goltz, Zühlsdorff and Wunderlich. All four had been questioned by Captain Wheatley and had subsequently made their final statements at the London Cage on 6 and 7 April. On the 25th, the day after Sir James Grigg's reply to the House of Commons, Mertens was charged and the following day, Steffan. Records do not state when the others were finally identified and charged although it is likely to have been during May or early June. In all, twelve prisoners were accused of Rosterg's murder, of whom eight eventually stood trial.

CHAPTER TWELVE

The London Trial

To your troops you can only offer one path
– the path that leads to Victory or Death.
Adolf Hitler to Field Marshal Rommel, 1942[1]

On 2 July 1945 a Military Court opened at the London Cage for the trial of eight German prisoners of war for murder. The initial indictments had called for twelve prisoners to face the charges but it appears that there was insufficient evidence on four of them – Bienek, Recksiek, Steffan and Jelinsky. Getting the remaining eight to court had been an achievement in itself. The first civilian investigators had met a complete 'wall of silence', and none of the many prisoners who must have witnessed what happened that night and morning were prepared, initially at least, to come forward. They would, after all, have been putting their own lives in danger. At the same time, some of them genuinely believed that Rosterg had been working for the British and thus deserved to be hanged as a traitor. This fundamental question – was Rosterg working to a British agenda? – would be raised again, and it still remains an unanswered question to this day.

The eight prisoners who were brought into court from their cells on the first floor of the London Cage were the four Waffen-SS men Kurt Zühlsdorff, Joachim Goltz, Erich Pallme Koenig and Heinz Brüling, the *Wehrmacht* soldiers Rolf Herzig and Hans Klein, the sailor Josef Mertens and the *Luftwaffe* man Herbert Wunderlich. The Military Court had been convened in the former dining-room, resplendent with its oak panelling, of 8 Kensington Palace Gardens. Military courts were a halfway house between a standard court martial and a civilian hearing. They were first introduced in the 'Regulations for the Maintenance of Discipline among Prisoners of War, 1939', to try by military court, prisoners and other non-British Army personnel for whom the King's Military Regulations did not pertain. Most military courts dealt with minor misdemeanours. Indeed, of the eleven previous cases all concerning Italian prisoners, eight were for minor misdemeanours, with the remaining three being for indecency.[2]

The presiding officer was Colonel R.H.A. Kellie and he was supported by five other officers, two lieutenant-colonels and three majors, who would ultimately decide the fate of the eight accused. The prosecuting officer was Major R.A.L. Hillard of the JAG's Office. (Later His Honour Richard Hillard MBE, he served as a Circuit Judge until 1972.) Defending the eight were two Army officers: Goltz, Brüling, Herzig and Mertens were represented by Major R. Evans, a solicitor, and Zühlsdorff, Pallme Koenig, Wunderlich and Klein by Captain Roger Willis who went on to serve as a Circuit Judge until 1981. Captain Willis was perhaps the more acceptable to the defendants because he too had been a prisoner of war, having been captured in North Africa while serving with the Middlesex Yeomanry. He had only returned from Germany three months beforehand. All eight were charged with 'Committing a civil offence, that is to say murder, in that they at Comrie on December 23rd, 1944, murdered Prisoner of War Number 788778 Feldwebel Wolfgang Rosterg'.[3] All pleaded not guilty.

Prior to hearing the case, the court was very keen to ensure strict fairness as only the British can. Two interpreters were provided by Colonel Scotland from the London Cage and they translated throughout. At the same time, the court also appreciated how hard it had been to find sufficient evidence to bring the case in the first place, owing to the intimidation of potential witnesses in Scotland. Consequently it was decided that all those who were to give evidence would not be named in court. It was hoped that this would conceal their identities in the subsequent media reports and thus ensure that the witnesses' families back in Germany could not be targeted in any way.

Flanked by tall Guards Brigade NCOs, the eight prisoners stood for the court opening and preliminary remarks by the president, Colonel Kellie. He explained the workings of the court and what the accused might expect to take place. He explained how proceedings would be longer than perhaps expected owing to the need to translate everything that was said, at the same time ensuring the prisoners fully understood all the implications of everything that was said. This they all nodded to and then took their seats.

Major Evans appeared first. He applied to the court for a separate trial for Brüling, because Brüling was to be called as a defence witness for Goltz and Mertens. 'One of the difficulties in this case,' he said, 'is to defend Brüling against himself and I feel that if I am going to use him as a witness in the defence of Goltz and Mertens then he should not be in the position of possibly convicting himself.'[4] Major Hillard opposed this, stating that they should all be tried jointly and that the trial would be fair. This was agreed to by the court, allowing the trial to begin. Hillard continued, outlining the case against the defendants. He described how Rosterg had arrived at Comrie on 22 December, the previous year, how he had been questioned as to his faith towards National Socialism, and how he had replied that he 'certainly was not'. Hillard then went on:

> Next morning at reveille, 6.30 a.m., in hut No. 4, there took place what might be described as a mock trial. Rosterg was standing there with a rope around his neck. The rope was being held by Koenig. A prisoner not before the court was reading from a document. Each allegation apparently was put to Rosterg bit by bit and he was expected to make a reply to each portion. He was repeatedly hit. Four of the accused hit him, one with an iron bar.
>
> Shortly before 8 o'clock the rope was removed from his neck and he was taken to a hut used by the Compound Leader. Inside the office there was what might be described as a summary hearing. Koenig told Rosterg that if he had any honour, he would hang himself. Rosterg replied that he was not able to do it. During the hearing, Koenig told the crowd outside that this 'swine' was going to hang himself and that if he didn't they knew what they had to do.
>
> The rope was then round Rosterg's neck. One end of it was seized by Goltz and Rosterg was thrown to the ground. He was kicked and stamped on. Rosterg was dragged by the rope 60 yards across the rough ground from the compound office into the lavatory. Goltz and Zühlsdorff put one end of the rope over a pipe which ran round the ceiling and Mertens pulled on the other end of the rope. Rosterg's body hung from the pipe with the feet off the ground and it was in that condition that he was found.[5]

Hillard then went on to say that in all probability, death occurred outside the camp office, not as a direct result of the hanging. Consequently, the prosecution's case was based on this.

The first witness called was Corporal Fritz Heubner. He gave his evidence as recounted previously. Interestingly enough, under questioning Heubner added that on at least one occasion, Pallme Koenig had taken Rosterg to the wash rooms during the initial questioning in Hut 4. This, he said, had been to wash the blood off his face and neck caused by the beatings with the iron bars. Once finished, Heubner had to endure cross-examination not only by the defence officers, but also by the accused themselves. This was a particular novelty of the military court system, ensuring complete impartiality and fairness. Mertens and Wunderlich declined to examine Heubner, but the others all tried to show that Heubner must have misidentified them. Herzig asked if Heubner could describe what he had been wearing that morning. Heubner replied, 'You wore an American pair of fatigue trousers with the letters "PW" on the seat in white.' Pallme Koenig asked a number of questions all designed to cast doubt on Heubner's identification of him both in Hut 4 and subsequently at the office of the Compound Leader. Heubner was not to be thrown, however. Pallme Koenig asked if Heubner was absolutely sure of his identification in both places. 'Yes.' Was he sure that it was Pallme Koenig who had held the rope which was around Rosterg's neck? 'I reiterate my statement,' replied Heubner, 'my memory is quite clear.' Pallme Koenig went on, 'Did you have a talk with me on the 23rd and on that day did you know me?' Heubner replied, 'I knew you because you used to come to my hut and you used to say that there was something fishy about me and you tried to find out about me.'[6] Answering questions put to him by the defending officers, Heubner went on to explain that he felt that even if Rosterg had been guilty of treachery, he should not have been murdered. He continued that since Rosterg's killing, he and others had felt very unsafe in the camp, to such an extent that they had requested a move. This had been granted although for one fellow prisoner it had been too late. He had been badly beaten.

During the first day of the trial only one witness was heard as most of the day was taken up with ensuring that the defendants understood exactly what was to happen. It was only on the subsequent days that the trial could really proceed. On 3 July three prosecution witnesses were heard before lunch: Charles Lergenmuller, Herman Bultmann (the compound booking in and out clerk at Devizes) and Wilhelm Schmidt who had been outside the compound office at Comrie. Lergenmuller's testimony was short and perhaps demonstrated the paucity of evidence that the investigating team had been able to find. In fact Lergenmuller was only called upon to identify Brüling as the man who had boasted to him in Comrie of having helped in the killing. This he did in short time. In turn, interestingly enough, Brüling said nothing. Only Klein asked a question of this witness, confirming that Lergenmuller was a former member of the Waffen-SS, as if perhaps trying to remind him of his ultimate loyalties.[7]

The evidence provided by Bultmann and Schmidt was much more thorough and initiated a string of questions from the defendants. Bultmann testified that he too had been under suspicion, having worked for the authorities in Devizes as a clerk. He stated that he had witnessed what took place in Hut 4 and the compound leader's hut, and that he had been forced to go to the latrines in front of the crowd dragging Rosterg there. He also recalled that Rosterg had been accused of being in contact with the French Resistance and police. Captain Willis questioned Bultmann first, having conferred with his 'clients' (those he was representing). He asked, 'Was it not a story which would be discreditable to a member of the German Armed Forces at the time?' Bultmann replied that anyone could have contact with the French civilian population at any time. Captain Willis went on to suggest to Bultmann that in fact it was Pallme Koenig he had witnessed conducting the proceedings against Rosterg in Hut 4. Pallme Koenig's questioning was brief and tried to show how, as a German soldier, he had been in no position to refuse to follow up the accusations levelled at Rosterg. 'Do you carry out orders by Germans while you are a prisoner of war?' Pallme Koenig asked. Bultmann bravely answered:

So far as the person who gives the orders has authority and so far as the orders do not conflict with morals and decency, but nowadays the situation is such that one must be ashamed to be a German.[8]

Both Goltz and Brüling tried to implicate Bultmann in the whole affair. Goltz suggested he had helped in pulling on the rope in the lavatory, while Brüling asked if he had not helped in dragging Rosterg there. 'No,' Bultmann replied, 'you took me by the collar and pushed me towards the lavatory.'[9]

Wilhelm Schmidt, the third witness that morning, had been present both outside the compound office and in the latrines where he had witnessed Rosterg's body being hanged. Schmidt's evidence was damning to Zühlsdorff, Brüling, Pallme Koenig, Herzig and Mertens. All of them, except Brüling, cross-examined him after Major Hillard had asked him to point out Mertens. (This would not have been difficult – everyone present knew that Mertens was the only naval defendant and consequently he was easy to identify as he was wearing a naval jacket. It must have clashed somewhat with his trousers – they were plum-coloured![10])

Zühlsdorff first tried to prove that Schmidt could not have been able to recognise him as it was still dark. The latter countered that everybody knew him and could recognise him through his tall stature and blond hair. Zühlsdorff then tried to implicate Schmidt as well: 'While Rosterg was being murdered did you feel pity for him?' 'I thought all the time,' replied Schmidt, 'how can these people kill a person? – I couldn't have done a thing like that.' Zühlsdorff continued, 'Why, then, did you say at some later date in the barracks in the evening, that Rosterg was a swine and that it served him right?' Schmidt parried this easily. He said:

> That is not true. At a later date when the camp leader read out a document which was supposed to be a copy of Rosterg's statement I said that if a man had done that it was not very nice but that we as prisoners of war had no authority to deal with the matter. Those in Germany ought to deal with it. I only said this because anybody who expressed views contrary to National Socialism would have suffered Rosterg's fate or been beaten up.[11]

Mertens's questioning of Schmidt was protracted. He asked repeated questions regarding each individual incident in which Schmidt had stated he had recognised Mertens as being involved. Then he also tried the now familiar technique of trying to implicate Schmidt. 'Did you have any opportunity to fetch help?' Mertens asked. Schmidt replied, 'I did not think about it at the time. Later I learned that anybody who interfered would have been clubbed to death, especially by members of the Afrika Korps in hut 6, with iron bars.' Mertens continued by asking Schmidt if he had not once stated that he would hang a known thief in the camp? 'No one was hanged,' replied Schmidt, 'but many said that whoever had stolen would get a good hiding.'

Goltz was next. He asked why, if Schmidt had felt so frightened, had he not requested to be transferred out of the camp? Schmidt answered, 'We had intended to ask the authorities to move us [but] other prisoners had found out about that and therefore we felt insecure.'[12]

Next Klein also tried to prove that Schmidt could not have recognised him for, as he claimed, no one really knew him in the camp. Schmidt refuted this, saying:

Some time before, which was a little time after you arrived in the camp, it was my duty to distribute the coal. One morning you came in a PW suit, the same as I am wearing now. You asked for coal for Hut 4 and I said that Hut 4 had already had its coal. You did not cut up rough but you did not get any coal either. Next day you came again, wearing your military decorations and I commented on your Knights' Cross and from that time on I remember you.[13]

Schmidt was also asked why he had not gone to the British authorities immediately, while things were still fresh in his mind concerning the events of that morning. He replied:

Anybody who wished to communicate with the British Authorities had to put a note in a mail box which was between two huts. This mail box was under constant observation by prisoners and it would have been far too dangerous to have put a note in it. I know on one occasion the mail box was torn down. People knew we wanted to get away from the camp and that was why we were summoned to a hut on the 25th January and one of us was badly beaten up.[14]

In the afternoon, Gefreiter Klaus Merfeld was called. He had been working alongside Wilhelm Schmidt at the coal yard on the morning of the killing. He stated that he and Schmidt had first gone to collect the coal buckets from each hut and then to the coal yard. Then they had gone to breakfast. All the time they had both heard various commotions but it was not until after breakfast that they had gone to the lavatory to investigate what was going on. Goltz and Mertens were the main two he had seen that morning; predictably they both tried to prove that either he had not seen them properly or that he was not even there because of his coal fatigues. Asked why he had not gone to fetch help or alert the authorities, Merfeld said, 'I did not know Rosterg; as regards the wash house, men have been taken there before when they have stolen something and have been given a dose of treatment, and were then let go'.[15] Merfeld's cross-examination carried over to the following day, 4 July. Both the defending officers questioned him, at the same time reminding him that the defendants' very lives depended on the evidence that he and the others gave. Merfeld stuck to his guns. He had truthfully recounted what he had seen.

On that day, the third day of the trial, the first British witness was called, an officer from the Intelligence Corps. Even in the records this individual's name was erased and so there is no indication as to his identity. His presence was required not only to inform the court about how the final defendants' statements were taken but also to refute some claims that the statements had been coerced from the prisoners and thus made under duress. Referred to as Captain X, the intelligence officer first described how statements had been taken from the defendants. Zühlsdorff's was then read out to the court by the Deputy Judge Advocate, Mr Stirling. Part of Zühlsdorff's statement said, 'I helped in the hanging in so far as I held Rosterg under the arms and lifted him up.' In another part it said, 'I heard a groaning from which I must assume that Rosterg was still alive.'[16] Mr Stirling also read out statements by Wunderlich and Brüling. Both had acknowledged that they had considered Rosterg a traitor but did not go so far as to admit that they had been involved in his murder. Both Goltz and Brüling then stated that they had been forced to write what they did. Both claimed that they had been told that a large number of witnesses had been found who would testify under oath to their involvement and that they might as well get used to the idea.

Major Evans went on to submit to the court that Goltz's statement, in particular, was inadmissible since it had been made as a result of inducement. Major Hillard, the prosecuting officer, contested this, saying that the stories of inducement were inconsistent. This was upheld.

On the morning of 5 July, the court heard the medical evidence concerning Rosterg. This was first given by the camp doctor and then by the doctor who had carried out the post-mortem. The rope used to hang Rosterg was introduced as an exhibit and it was demonstrated how it had fitted around Rosterg's neck. The camp medical officer, an unidentified major in the RAMC, stated what had happened once medical help reached Rosterg:

> The rope had been taken from the neck. Artificial respiration was being conducted. I listened for heart sounds and decided that there was some audible sound and it was not at all certain that he was dead. I satisfied myself later on that he was dead before I abandoned artificial respiration.

The second medical witness testified that Rosterg's head and face had extensive bruising, with injuries to the eyes and ears that were consistent with having been hit with a heavy stick or iron bar. However, these injuries were not serious enough to have caused death. The rope exhibit was then passed across to the medical witness and he confirmed that this rope had fitted the constriction marks around the neck very well. In his opinion, therefore, it was likely that death had been caused by strangulation which must have been quite sudden. The Deputy Judge Advocate General then asked if it could be deduced whether death had occurred before or after Rosterg had been hung up from the pipe in the latrine. The witness stated that death had been consistent with strangulation and not with hanging, therefore in his opinion, Rosterg had died before he was strung up.[17]

These statements ended the case for the prosecution. Now midway through the trial, it seemed that a number of points rested solely on hearsay. Of course, in July 1945 there was very little forensic evidence of the type that we have come to expect, even rely on, today. Consequently, Captain Willis submitted to the court that there really was no *prima facie* case against either Klein or Wunderlich. Mr

Stirling then declared that he agreed that the case against Klein was not sufficiently proved and that he was to be found not guilty and released back into custody as a normal prisoner of war, although he was to remain in the building during the rest of the trial. As regards Wunderlich, however, he felt that there had been sufficient evidence to warrant his continued trial. This did not necessarily mean he was guilty, though.

With Klein removed, the case continued. Each of the seven remaining defendants had all elected to give evidence, and it was at this point that they really condemned themselves. Zühlsdorff was the first to address the court. He stated that on 10 May, while still in Comrie, he had overheard some of the other POWs discussing the case and that they had declared that it was Brüling or Goltz who had killed Rosterg. He had been interviewed twice at Devizes and then again on 25 March at Comrie. He was convinced that he had been betrayed by somebody and that all traitors must die.

Continuing his evidence the following day, 6 July, Zühlsdorff stated that he was from the Waffen-SS. Questioned by Major Hillard as to whether he was also 'a good Nazi', Zühlsdorff had replied, 'If I am an SS man then I am also a National Socialist.'[18] He went on:

> I would have helped in the hanging of Rosterg in any case because he was a traitor, but I should not have taken orders from Koenig. Men outside the office were saying that the traitor had betrayed German Red Cross helpers and German signal personnel women. I was very disgusted.[19]

Zühlsdorff continued by saying that in London, while being held at the Cage, Goltz had told him that he had thrown Rosterg to the ground and knelt on him. Asked by Major Hillard whether he had been quite prepared to assist in the killing of Rosterg, Zühlsdorff replied, 'Yes, to hang him as it is fitting for a traitor.' The Deputy Judge Advocate then asked what evidence was there that Rosterg had betrayed people? Zühlsdorff replied:

> Not only one comrade of mine but many told me that these notes and drawings were made by Rosterg . . . had only one or up to five people told me about these things against Rosterg, I should not have believed them because that might have been a purely personal association, but as 20 to 30 people in the barracks were talking about these things, I did believe

them. This man was a traitor and he deserved death by the rope. I helped because the man was too heavy for my comrades to pull him up. I would just as well have helped if this man had still been alive. The object was that we could maintain afterwards that he had hanged himself. This man had to be found hanging because that is the righteous death of a traitor.[20]

Wunderlich also gave evidence in his defence that day. He stated that he had served for three and a half years in the *Luftwaffe* and that an escape plan he had put together at Devizes had been betrayed. He also agreed that traitors should be hanged: 'The correct punishment is the rope which is the same in every land,' he stated.

Herzig, too, spoke of the Devizes escape plan having been betrayed. With regards to being a Nazi, Herzig said, 'As soon as you become a front-line soldier, politics play no part. I never hit Rosterg, nor did I do anything to Rosterg that could have led to his death.'[21] Herzig went on to declare that he had been told by Klein that Rosterg was a traitor. Since Klein wore the Knights' Cross, there was no reason to doubt him. When asked by Major Hillard whether he had believed Klein, Herzig said:

At a time like that one remembered the English proverb, 'Right or Wrong, my Country'. So I said 'that man deserves the rope' . . . had I been in a proper physical state to have done that I have no doubt that I should have been led that way . . . because I should have liked to see how a hanging traitor looked . . . I wanted to see what such a monstrosity looked like.[22]

Pallme Koenig also briefly gave evidence that day. He stated that he had been in the same hut as Rosterg and that on the night of 22 December, after a brief struggle, documents had been taken from Rosterg that 'would have made any German angry'. It was also impossible for Rosterg to have run away, he went on, since all the doors were locked at night. Had he got out he would have been shot by the guards without warning.[23]

The next day being Sunday, the court was adjourned until 9 July. It was now the turn of Josef Mertens, the naval corporal, to give evidence. Like the others, he was soon condemning himself as he described Rosterg's body being dragged to the latrines:

It was clear to me that he [was] the traitor and it was also clear that the man was dead. I seized the rope and helped to pull it for the last few yards to the pipe. I assisted in hanging up the body. Rosterg had himself admitted that he was a traitor. I certainly thought that he deserved the rope and said so at the time. Anyone who had suffered the aerial attacks at home understood why we were incensed against the traitor . . . we left him there because he was already dead. I was of the opinion that a traitor should be found hanging.[24]

Goltz's evidence before the court was even more damaging. He made no effort to try and hide his guilt. Standing very upright he calmly told the court what had happened in Hut 4 once he had seen his name on the list of prisoners taken from Rosterg:

The crowd was very enraged and knew absolutely that it was the question of a traitor and kept shouting 'Hang up the swine'. I myself became incensed and excited and saw a traitor before me. At this moment I completely lost my self-control and saw red. I became even more incensed when I realised that through this man I had been suspected of being a traitor myself. That was a question of my own military honour . . . [Outside the compound office] I took hold of the rope in my hand and pulled the noose tight around Rosterg's neck, pulled the traitor to the ground and knelt upon him and pulled the noose tight again. The crying stopped when I knelt on Rosterg and pulled the rope tight. I assumed at this moment he died. The rope was taken out of my hand and Rosterg was pulled away from under me.[25]

Thus ended the case for the defence.

★ ★ ★

The following two days were spent in hearing the final statements by all three British officers, as well as the final summing up by the Deputy Judge Advocate General. Major Evans declared that the motive was revenge against a traitor. He went on:

There can be no doubt that there was a motive for the killing of Rosterg. There were in the [compound] at Comrie about 900 prisoners and they were true to their loyalty of their uniform and they had exactly the same motive.[26]

Continuing, Major Evans surmised that the evidence concerning

Brüling showed insufficient grounds on which he could be found guilty of murder. In the case of Goltz, he asked the court to consider whether he really was guilty of murder or should instead be charged with the lesser offence of manslaughter, stating:

> Goltz is a man who has been brought up with certain loyalties and traditions and he is very jealous of his honour as a soldier. He did what he did with ample provocation to reduce the charge from one of murder to manslaughter.[27]

Major Evans went on to state that if Goltz were to be found guilty of manslaughter and the others were found guilty along with him, they too could only be found guilty of manslaughter.

Records of the final statement by Captain Willis and the summing up by Mr Stirling do not seem to have survived. It is recorded that the Deputy Judge Advocate instructed the court only to consider three possible verdicts: guilty of murder, guilty of manslaughter or not guilty. Dressed in his wig and gown, Mr Stirling said:

> I am going to suggest that from the German point of view, Rosterg was not a good soldier and that he would have deserved and received from any good German contempt and dislike. You will probably think he deserted from the German Army, not merely by leaving it so that he might spend his time as he liked, but deserted to the enemy – the British.[28]

The verdicts on the seven men still before the court were delivered the same day, 12 July 1945. Wunderlich was found not guilty but the remaining six were found guilty of murder. Throughout the trial, it was often noted by those present that some of the defendants, Zühlsdorff, Brüling and Pallme Koenig in particular, had given the appearance of boredom, slouching in their chairs and often doodling in their notebooks. It was only towards the end of the trial, when they realised that they faced the death penalty, that they sat straighter in their chairs and paid attention. It was too late. After due deliberation, Zühlsdorff, Brüling, Pallme Koenig, Mertens and Goltz were sentenced to death by hanging. Herzig was more lucky – he was sentenced to penal servitude for life with hard labour.

That same day, Erich Pallme Koenig wrote a note to Lieutenant-Colonel Alexander Scotland at the London Cage. It had been

Scotland who had persuaded the defendants to accept British defending officers who would know the intricacies of British law. Pallme Koenig wrote:

> After the end of our trial and most likely the end of our stay here, I should like in the name of my comrades and in my own name, to express to you, Sir, our gratitude. Due to your advice we asked for British Officers to be assigned to us for our defence and we have been agreeably surprised. Without your advice we would, most likely, have made a different choice.
>
> Due to your and the major's instructions, our stay here had been alleviated, we were allowed to work and time passed relatively quickly.
>
> I beg to be allowed to ask you a favour. When we are being sent away from here, we would be grateful to you, Sir, if we were not sent to a camp where we would have to wait from one empty day to another, but could help to rebuild the destroyed parts of London. If it should not be possible for us to work together, I beg to ask to be transferred to an Austrian PW Camp.
>
> I beg to let me tell you this myself and to be convinced that even after our return to our homes we shall be pleased to remember your personality, Sir, and that of the Major.

Erich Pallme Koenig
Oberfahnrich[29]

CHAPTER THIRTEEN

Just Desserts

Nothing can be more solemn or impressive
than a military execution.
J. MacMullen, *Camp and Barrack Room*, 1846[1]

Although five of the German prisoners were duly sentenced to death, there were some legal questions that still had to be answered. In a note to the Judge Advocate General, the DPW wrote on 18 July:

> As you know, Article 66 of the Convention provides that where sentence of death is passed, notice must be given to the Protecting Power for transmission to the Power in whose Armed Forces the prisoner of war served. Sentence shall not be carried out until at least 3 months have expired from the date of this notice . . .
>
> The question arises whether, under present circumstances, Article 66 applies, and whether 3 months must elapse before the sentence of death, if confirmed, is carried out.
>
> In my view, Article 66 . . . can no longer be applied. There is no Protecting Power for German interests in the United Kingdom and in any event there is no German Government to whom notice could be transmitted.
>
> The Foreign Office have been consulted and agree with the above view.
>
> I understand that you wished to be informed as soon as possible of my views and those of the Foreign Office on this matter in order that you could deal with the point when advising on confirmation.[2]

On 23 July the Judge Advocate General wrote to the General Commanding London District at Leconfield House in Curzon Street, confirming the court's verdict. In his letter, he also referred to a petition submitted by the six prisoners against the findings of the court and the sentence of death. He wrote:

> I have considered the petition, in conjunction with the Proceedings of trial. I am of opinion that there was evidence to support the convictions

for murder in the case of the six Prisoners of War, and that the sentences of death by hanging are legally in order.

In my opinion, the petition discloses no legal grounds for withholding confirmation of those proceedings.

While German Prisoners of War are within the King's Peace the justification which they advance in the Petition affords no defence. They are not entitled to take the law into their own hands, or to create a breach of such Peace.

I am of opinion that these Proceedings may be confirmed.

The sentences of death are, however, matters for the military authorities . . .[3]

Unfortunately, the prisoners' petition does not seem to have survived in the records. Either way, it had now become irrelevant. After the letter from the Judge Advocate General confirming sentence, it was up to the Officer Commanding the District to decide finally the fate of the guilty. There was still one final hurdle, however, before the sentences could be finally confirmed and carried out. As with all cases of execution, all the papers of the proceedings of the trial had to be submitted to the King 'for the signification of his Pleasure thereon'. King George signed.

It is not clear from the archives where those sentenced to death were housed for the next three months. It is likely they were kept at Pentonville Prison in London which had been taken over by the military at the beginning of the war. Either way, on 5 October 1945 Mr Albert Pierrepoint, the Chief Executioner, arrived at Pentonville to inspect the five men who were to be executed the following morning, 6 October, starting at 9 o'clock.

Albert Pierrepoint was very much the professional. He would always observe beforehand those he was about to hang. This was in order to ensure that they dropped the correct distance, giving a clean break of the neck, and avoiding strangulation through dropping too short a distance, and decapitation through dropping too far. The five prisoners were seen by Pierrepoint in the exercise yard that evening. Of the prisoners he recalled the following:

They looked like ordinary people, only lads, you know; I suppose they looked a bit despondent . . . knowing where they were going and what was going to happen to them. There's nobody knows, only them, what they're feeling like.

We started at nine o'clock in the morning, and those five would take about three hours . . . you have to alter every drop of fall . . . it all depends on the weight – if he gets a long drop it'd pull his head off, decapitate him.[4]

Promptly at 9 o'clock that morning, the executions began. Most newspapers reported the executions but there were not many bystanders outside the gates of the prison. As was the custom, a notice of execution was duly posted on the doors. It read:

DECLARATION OF SHERIFF
AND OTHERS

We, the undersigned, hereby declare that Judgement of Death was this day executed on Karl Zühlsdorff, Josef Mertens, Joachim Goltz, Heinz Brüling, Erich Pallme Koenig in His Majesty's Prison of Pentonville in our presence. Dated this 6th day of October 1945
Lt-Col F. Forbes – Deputy Provost Marshal London District
Ben Grew – Governor
Ronald George Smith & Clifford Howell (RC) – Chaplains to the Forces

Later a medical certificate was also posted up on the door, signed by Mr Herbert P. Young, the prison surgeon, stating that he had examined the bodies and declared them dead. The executions were noted by many papers as having been the largest multiple hanging since 1883, when those found guilty of the Phoenix Park murders in Dublin had also been hanged. What the papers did not know, however, was that there had been a serious problem immediately after the sentences were carried out. Albert Pierrepoint again:

I remember one of them had a gold medal on – a chain and a gold medal. And I had three assistants that day, and they were all saying, 'I'd like that for a souvenir'. Anyway, after the executions were over, the officer came round; now he says, 'One of these men – prisoners – had a medal round his neck with a gold chain and it's missing, have any of you got it? No, they all [said] they hadn't. So the officer went and got all the soldiers there, 12 or 14 soldiers, and he had them all in a line. He says, 'Now, as you know this certain man had a . . . gold chain on . . . he'd been brave in battle or something like that. Now the man who's got that medal . . . just step one step rearward.' Nobody spoke. 'For the last time . . . admit you've got it, hand it back, it won't go any further; otherwise there will be a lot of trouble.' And one man stepped out, pulled it out of his pocket and gave it in. So it shows, you see.[5]

★ ★ ★

The military court that found the prisoners guilty was not the only one to hear evidence on the Rosterg murder. On 29 August 1945 a second military court was convened at 8 Kensington Palace Gardens to bring to trial on a lesser charge of manslaughter those prisoners acquitted of murder at the first trial and those who had not appeared at all. Both Klein and Wunderlich were present, alongside Recksiek, Jelinsky, Bienek and Laise. There seem to be no surviving records of this case, nor indeed did the newspapers seem at all interested. The only reference to it appears in Colonel Scotland's own papers, now in the Public Record Office. These contain a curious note written by Bienek to Goeckel, who was still at Comrie, on 22 September. (Goeckel was the man who had been named by two German officers, interviewed by CSDIC, as the leader of the Nazis in the camp and the man who was orchestrating the majority of the intimidation.) Barely two weeks before the executions were to be carried out, Bienek was still trying to contact his spiritual mentor, Goeckel, in Scotland. There is no supporting record stating how the note was discovered or by whom, nor even where. It read:

GOECKEL and comrades!!!

Comrades and chums!
The prosecutor has demanded the death sentence against our 5 comrades. This was the harshest he could ask for. The verdict has not yet been promulgated, but is not likely to be very mild. Keep on the look out as the verdict will be announced in the next few days. . . . SKRUPKE is to be my defending council. In his opinion they can't tie anything on me, if there is even a shadow of justice . . . Always *burn* notes! And don't speak conspicuously, as I have already been told off by the Commandant. The newspaper containing the verdict is extremely important!!! Perhaps you can still get hold of an old paper of Tuesday or Wednesday, in which the case for the defence appears, either in full or in part!!! Are Hans KLEIN or WUNDERLICH with you? They should send us a detailed report! Have RECKSIEK and JELINSKY already applied for the permission to speak to SKRUPKE? As I now live on the floor below yours we could establish an

'air mail' with thread during fog and darkness. No. 10 has three windows
. . . take your bearings from the lamp standard in the barbed-wire fence
. . . WUNDERLICH can take the biggest risks as we do not need him as a
witness and, after all, he has already been acquitted.[6]

This note gives the impression that Wunderlich and Klein were
acquitted a second time, but the verdicts on the others cannot be
ascertained. The mention of a German defending officer must
have meant that the accused did not choose a British Officer this
time, despite what Pallme Koenig had written. Perhaps they did
not know.

So there ended the final act of the Devizes Plot and the murder of
Feldwebel Wolfgang Rosterg. It is certainly a remarkable story. But
did anything good come out of such a tragedy? The answer is
probably yes. The Rosterg murder provided the much needed
impetus to the screening and segregation programmes. This in turn
allowed ordinary prisoners to get on with their lives, especially in late
1945, when they had a lot to come to terms with: that Hitler was
dead and that Germany had lost the war; that their country had
committed genocide, not only against the Jews but also against the
less fortunate in their own society; that their country was destroyed
and one half of it occupied by the Russians. And all this had come
about in only eleven months – since 6 June 1944.

Rosterg's murder was not the only one, however. One prisoner
was beaten to death in Sheffield by other prisoners, while several
others were shot trying to escape. After 8 May – VE Day – the
German POW population had more important things to think
about than upholding National Socialist ideals. Men like Herbert
Sulzbach were needed more than ever now, to lead the confused,
bewildered prisoners through the realisation that Germany had lost
the war. Final defeat was crushing. As late as April 1945, prisoners
in Comrie were writing to the Führer in Germany on his birthday.
Bruno Rikall in Comrie wrote:

My Führer
On your 56th birthday I wish to send in my name, and in the name of all
comrades of Camp 21 and Compound D, our best birthday regards. We
all hope that our Lord may give you, our Führer, strength and health to
lead our army to a glorious victory and a just peace. May you continue to

lead our beloved native land to peaceful recovery. Although with hands
bound, our hearts believe in you, my Führer!
   Heil Hitler![7]

Hans Mildner, also at Comrie, wrote on behalf of all the prisoners:

On the occasion of the 56th birthday of our Führer, we send you with our
birthday regards a donation of RM 327,230 in the name of all the
German soldiers of Camp 21 as a sign of our unbroken loyalty to our
Führer and our nation, as a birthday present for our beloved Führer.
   We think about our brave German homeland, and we are sure that we
shall gain a heroic victory in spite of very great misfortune.
   Long Live the Führer; Long Live Greater Germany.
   Heil Hitler![8]

But these letters, as well as many more like them, were never to reach
Germany – the postal system had failed long before. Then came the
surrender. Many of the prisoners simply refused to believe that it had
happened, instead choosing to believe that what they were told was
mere Allied propaganda. Sulzbach himself wrote, '60% of our 4,000
POW here don't believe that Germany has surrendered'.[9]
   Often those who began to accept the truth were intimidated by
others. Herbert Sulzbach recorded just such an incident:

After the surrender of the German Armies in Italy, I gathered a number
of POWs around a radio and asked them to listen to the BBC. A German
NCO switched it on. The announcer told the audience of the surrender.
Shortly after, the German NCO who had switched on the radio came to
my office and asked for protective custody because his fellow POWs were
threatening him as a collaborator, claiming that 'of course, the BBC
announcer was a fake'.
   I visited the POWs who were in protective custody every day and
brought them food and literature. One of these soldiers told me that Hitler
had a tiny bomb with which an entire city could be destroyed. Only later I
realised that he had been talking about a German atom bomb.[10]

Herbert Sulzbach worked tirelessly at Comrie to try to break the Nazi
hold on the camp. He issued circular after circular to the prisoners as
well as bombarding the Political Intelligence Department at the
Foreign Office with suggestions. In June 1945 he faced his ultimate
challenge – the truth about the concentration camps. It had been

decided by the Allied powers that every prisoner of war was to see the films and photographs taken at some of these camps, showing the full horrors of what had happened over so many years. First a pamphlet was produced by the British Ministry of Information showing what had been found at Belsen and copies were distributed to each hut. Sulzbach wrote:

> The response to the photos and my comments was interesting and gratifying. Many of the POWs came into my office, horrified by what they had seen. Yet there were quite a number of prisoners who believed the photographs were fakes. 'Made in Hollywood,' some exclaimed. At first this made me angry. But thinking it over I became convinced that their disbelief was a positive sign: they just could not believe that such cruelties were possible or had been committed in the name of Germany.[11]

Soon after, Sulzbach began to notice a profound difference in the prisoners. They started to believe what they were being told. Sulzbach was lucky, also, in that he was fully supported by Colonel Wilson in the matter of re-education. Henry Faulk, the Chief Executive Officer for PWE, visited Comrie on his rounds of the camps and he at once endorsed the work by Colonel Wilson and Herbert Sulzbach. Indeed, he was so impressed with Sulzbach that he urged him to put in for a commission. Fittingly, Sulzbach was promoted lieutenant in December 1945 just after his biggest single 'victory' at Comrie. Just before the annual Remembrance Sunday (11 November) that year, Sulzbach had urged the prisoners to remember their own dead. He asked them to parade of their own free will at eleven o'clock on 11 November 1945. Almost the entire camp turned out. Herbert Sulzbach wrote proudly of that moment:

> Out of the 4,000 German POWs only about a dozen stayed, like Ajax, sulking in their huts. On a raw November morning the remainder stood to attention on the football field, while the 'Last Post' was sounded. My satisfaction was that Nazism could be fought and beaten as early as 1945.[12]

In December 1945 Sulzbach left Comrie for Camp 18, an officers' camp at Featherstone Park in Northumberland, where he was soon promoted to Captain. (Herbert Sulzbach was in fact, the first man to

have held both a German and a British Commission.) Sulzbach was
to remain with the German prisoners until the very last ones were
repatriated in 1948. When the German Embassy reopened in the
1950s, he worked tirelessly for the Anglo-German Friendship Society
as well as for a United Europe and was to work with six German
Ambassadors during their postings to London.

The camp Sulzbach left behind that December bore very little
relation to the camp of six months previously. As early as June 1945,
it was being reported on favourably by those whose job it was to
oversee the re-education programmes. One of the first visits came
between 20 and 26 June and was conducted by James Grant. His
report began:

> In spite of the bad reputation that this camp has, I found the atmosphere
> good, and an agreeable absence of tension, which I attribute to the
> Commandant, Lt-Col A.K. Wilson. When POWs talked about letters
> never coming from their homes, they said that the delay must be
> elsewhere, because the Commandant was so fair that he would never
> punish a man in this way; they mentioned, however, that if they stepped
> off the straight and narrow path he could be very severe.[13]

By now Comrie had four compounds, A to D, with its satellite labour
camp (Camp 21A) still at Cowden, commanded by Major Paget.
Each compound contained some 900 prisoners and there were a
further 750 or so at Cowden. Grant's report centred on the quality
and standards that were being achieved in the teaching of English
and also reported on the suitability of the camp for a full re-
education programme. This he fully endorsed, his only real
complaint being that there were not enough pencils for the prisoners
to write with! By July, outside lecturers were visiting the camp,
including one Doctor von Waldheim whose talks to the prisoners
were regarded very highly, although his subject is not recorded.
Colonel Wilson, however, was concerned that only some 250
prisoners could attend at any one time. Mr H. King, the Director of
Lectures at PID, urged him not to worry as his lecturers were 'quite
experienced and relatively tough people and . . . we could ask them
to give four, or even five, lectures per day'.[14]

By August 1945 Comrie was very different. All the 'Blacks' had now been screened out and moved to Camp 165, while the 'Greys' had 'gone south'. Standards of English had improved as had the reception of other re-education programmes. By December Mr King was reporting:

> There is little change at Comrie since my last visit. The change of Commandant and Interpreter (Lt.-Col. Wilson & S/Sgt Sulzbach) were referred to as almost personal grief by the Ps/W but in my opinion the result will be good . . . the further period of individual re-adjusting will now take place. Now they have to stand on their own feet.[15]

Comrie eventually closed as a POW Camp in 1947, but it is still used today as an occasional Army training camp.

But what of Devizes? Le Marchant Camp also continued to house prisoners up until 1947. But it differed from most other camps in that it became the POW Medical Training School, also part of the re-education programme. Camp 23, Devizes, closed in April 1946, and was taken over by 410 German PW Working Camp. The new Commandant, Lieutenant-Colonel K.J.P. Oliphant MC, was reportedly from the same mould as Colonel Wilson at Comrie. He was very keen to ensure that re-education achieved its goals and had personally directed his new Intelligence Officer, Lieutenant Lootens, to involve himself more with re-education tasks than with the more normal POW tasks of such a position.

A report written on 12 April 1946 said that morale at Devizes was quite good, except for that of 500 prisoners who had recently arrived from America. These men were reported as having 'lost their former discipline; this is being tackled'.[16] Unfortunately, at the time of the inspection very little had happened at Devizes as regards re-education prior to the closing of Camp 23 and the opening of 410 German PW Working Camp. Also, it was noted, there had been very little screening although the camp population was now only some 2,000 strong. By the end of April, the camp strength had fallen even further, to just 1,738, of whom just under half were still graded as 'C' or 'C-plus'. There were even forty practising Communists reported 'but they do not cut much ice'. The pro-Nazi standing of the camp was blamed squarely on those who had come from America. The May 1946 report stated:

[The] recent influx of about 488 P/W from the USA, mainly tough types captured in North Africa, makes the present complexion Grey/Black and has a depressing influence on the remaining P/W, who resent their presence. They retard the excellent progress already made on re-education . . . These men are arrogant and extremely insolent and openly state their preference for National Socialism, leaving interrogators no option but to grade them C+.[17]

Arthur McKechnie was stationed in Le Marchant Barracks between April 1946 and January 1948. He was almost sixteen years old when he moved to Devizes from his home town of Hungerford. He joined the re-formed band of the Second Battalion, Royal Wiltshire Regiment. The original band had gone to France with the battalion, many of its members never to return. With so many troops still abroad, bands were very much in demand for the numerous ceremonial as well as social gatherings that were now expected to take place both at home and abroad. For Arthur McKechnie, joining into 'boy-service', the daily routine was rather more educational and sporting than military. Mr McKechnie recalled those days:

The barracks were almost deserted at that time, and only housed a very small depot party of the Wiltshire Regiment and the recently re-formed band of the Second Battalion . . . This was long before the barracks were turned into an Infantry Training Centre and later the 62nd Primary Training Centre mainly for the Wessex Brigade regiments.

The barracks perimeter joined Le Marchant Camp, the large German Prisoner of War camp. By the early part of 1946, things in general had become very relaxed; although guards still patrolled, it was very easy for prisoners to escape and they very often did. On many occasions POWs escaped through 'their' wire into the barracks to steal eggs from the hen houses in the gardens of the Officers' Mess. Often it was a case of who got there first – the prisoners or the Band Boys!

German POWs were employed as cooks by the Wiltshire Regiment at the depot, one of them having been a top cake-maker in civilian life and often delighted us all with an exquisite delicacy – a welcome change from the normal 'slab' cake.

The first party of German POWs to be returned to Germany left on the same day as the band . . . both left by different trains from Devizes station and travelled to Harwich, then via the Hook of Holland, to Germany.[18]

By August 1946 the situation at Devizes was reported as having improved considerably. This was primarily because some repatriations had started and many of those initially graded as C+ had been downgraded and separated from the real 'Blacks'. In fact the majority of the camp was reported as being non-political, with 25 per cent being classed as 'democrats', 20 per cent 'mostly youngsters' and only 3–4 per cent true National Socialists. The Communist element had vanished![19]

By the end of 1946, Camp 410 was hardly recognisable. In an undated letter to DPW, Mr P.F. Doring, a camp inspector for PWD, wrote:

> The Commandant, Colonel Oliphant, is the finest type of professional British Officer, the type of Christian gentleman. The work he has done and is doing is simply splendid and the change he has brought about since he took over is astounding . . .
>
> There are beautiful flower beds in the camp, there are merry fountains, there is a model windmill with all sorts of devices, there are bee hives . . . and all this is stimulated by the Colonel who is assisted by a splendid team of officers . . .
>
> I saw piles of barbed wire outside the camp. 'Our' Colonel ordered it to be pulled down with the result that there is an atmosphere of trust, even happiness . . .[20]

Camp 410 closed in February 1947 and so ended the Devizes link with German prisoners of war, save those, however, who elected to continue to live in Britain. Most of these men did so because their homelands had been overrun by the Russians or had been handed back to the Poles. In Wiltshire alone, the author met seven of these men, now happily fulfilling the role of grandfathers. They still take pride in being German and having served as soldiers, sailors or submariners for their country, but not their party. Indeed, the majority are now more English than those around them, their local accents thicker. Their stories and memories are legion.

But what of the British side of this remarkable tale? PWIS(H), under its indefatigable leader, Colonel Alexander Scotland, was disbanded and then reborn as the War Crimes Interrogation Unit (WCIU) in December 1945. It became primarily responsible for identifying, locating and interrogating wanted war criminals both for the Nuremberg Trials as well as for the numerous smaller trials held by the Allied nations. During this period, from December 1945 to the middle of 1948, some 3,573 prisoners of war and civilians passed through the London Cage. Colonel Scotland and his team were responsible for submitting over a thousand statements on such cases as the murder of British prisoners at Paradis and Wormhout in 1940, the Stalag Luft III murders and even the killings of hundreds of Russian slave labourers in the Channel Islands. The final reports were written in November 1948, prior to the Cage's closure. Nos 6 and 8 Kensington Palace Gardens were demolished in the Sixties and replaced with glass monstrosities.

As for CSDIC, it too was wound up. Wilton Park closed at the end of 1945 and was redesignated the Headquarters for re-education. Selected prisoners were trained there on two-month courses prior to being posted to other camps to help in the re-education process. In all, some 300 prisoners passed through Wilton Park until it was also closed in 1948. Like the London Cage, the original house has long since been demolished to make way for another monstrosity that now houses the accommodation of the British Army School of Languages.

Today, Wolfgang Rosterg's remains lie buried in the German Military Cemetery at Cannock Chase in Staffordshire. He lies alongside Major Willi Thorn. Together, they represent the unfortunate legacy of all that was evil in the German Prisoner of War camps in Britain and elsewhere. But in hindsight, their deaths and those of others, were not meaningless: they spurred on the Allied authorities to cleanse the world of Hitler and National Socialism. Today, Germany is again united and has for some time been a central power in Europe. She is well aware of her new legacy and, God willing, she will never forget it.

Postscript

There remains one unanswered question about the death of Wolfgang Rosterg. Why was he sent to Camp 21? Comrie was known for its hard, 'Black' nature and although prisoners such as Zühlsdorff, Goltz and Pallme Koenig may have felt at home there, for the likes of Rosterg it was a virtual death sentence. Other authors have suggested a variety of reasons. Some claim that the evidence points to Rosterg as working for the British, perhaps even for MI19. This is very unlikely as Rosterg would be well known to those who also came up from Devizes. His very nature, his open rejection of National Socialism, would have precluded his selection for such a task by an organisation which was, if nothing else, highly professional and just would not use such an outspoken personality. In fact, throughout the whole war, only forty-nine 'stoolies' were ever recruited and used, a demonstrative fact in itself. Neither Storch nor Wunderlich were 'stoolies' in the true sense, since they had not been trained for the job. Yet Wunderlich was the real traitor. He talked to save his own position and then went on to blame Rosterg, an easy target because of his criticisms of Hitler and National Socialism. The British authorities knew this, which is probably why Wunderlich faced a second trial.

Others have suggested that Rosterg may not have been so innocent while at Devizes. A recent book claimed that one of the escapes from Devizes in November 1944 was made using a pair of wire-cutters obtained from the work room of the Clerk of Works, Jim Gaiger. Rosterg would have been, probably, the only man with such ready access. Perhaps his anti-Nazi views, so openly displayed, were a smokescreen? Again, this is doubtful. The most likely reason for Rosterg's going to Comrie was apathy. He went because the others went. It was easy; all the authorities had to do was put them all on a train and the problem would be solved – or so they thought. His death was but one single tragedy in six years of tragedies.

Another theory that has been postulated is that of the planned mass break-outs from a number of camps and the combined advance to the east coast and/or attack on London. This is absurd since there is no evidence to support this today or in the past. In December 1944 Hitler was looking at the Ardennes, and nothing would be allowed to jeopardise his plans. Certainly, he did not have the resources to squander on futile missions to England. If he had not been able to invade in 1940 or 1941, he was not going to contemplate any form of manpower-intensive operations there in 1944.

With the benefit of hindsight, it is very easy to criticise the British handling of the Devizes situation. That being said, the Axis prisoners in Britain, Canada and America certainly endured a far more humane existence than their fellow countrymen held prisoner in the Soviet Union, or the Allied prisoners in Germany and Japan. They did not have to endure the constant mental battering that was imposed on the United Nations' prisoners in North Korea or China. They did not have to endure the complete degradation suffered by the French and Americans in North Vietnam. Nor did they die in their thousands, herded into cattle sheds and shot, some after prolonged torture, as has happened so recently in the former Yugoslavia. No, the prisoners in Allied hands, on the whole, had a relatively easy time of it. For this they must owe an enormous debt of gratitude to the likes of the Sulzbachs and Colonel Wilsons of that time, who upheld the good that lay beneath the Allied cause, and continued to uphold it after the victory.

★ ★ ★

Today, there is little left in Devizes of the huge wooden barracks that once lined the London Road. Le Marchant Barracks is still standing, momentarily safe from Treasury axes and housing speculators. But of the POW camps, very little survives, except for several large Romney huts, recently re-skinned and now occupied by the machinery and stores of the local council roads department.

In Comrie, unlike Devizes, the majority of Camp 21 still remains. Used primarily as a local cadre and TA training camp, it still retains a small military staff overseeing the area. Local rumour has it that Major Willi Thorn still haunts the hut where he died, forever tormented by the cruelty he endured at the hands of his so-called comrades.

Notes

Chapter One

1. Lieutenant-Colonel A.P. Scotland, *The London Cage* (Evans Brothers Ltd, London, 1957), p. 15
2. Ibid, p. 16
3. Ibid, p. 17
4. Ibid, p. 18
5. Ibid, p. 28
6. Ibid, p. 32
7. Ibid, p. 34
8. Ibid, p. 39
9. Imperial War Museum (IWM) Sound Archive Interview: Herbert Sulzbach 4338/3
10. Everett Archive: Sulzbach Papers
11. Ibid
12. IWM Sulzbach interview
13. Ibid
14. Matthew Barry Sullivan, *Thresholds of Peace* (Hamish Hamilton, London, 1979), p. 62
15. Everett Archive: Sulzbach Papers
16. Ibid
17. IWM Sulzbach interview
18. Ibid
19. Ibid
20. *Thresholds of Peace*, p. 63
21. *The London Cage*, p. 50
22. Ibid, p. 52
23. Ibid, p. 53
24. Ibid, p. 54
25. Ibid, pp. 65–6

Chapter Two

1. R. Kipling, *Barrack Room Ballads*, 1902
2. *The London Cage*, p. 66
3. For a much more comprehensive account, the reader should study F.H. Hinsley *et al.*, *British Intelligence in the Second World War*, vol. 1 (HMSO, London, 1979), p. 288
4. M.R.D. Foot & J.M. Langley, *MI9 Escape and Evasion 1939–1945* (The Bodley Head, London, 1979), p. 34
5. Ibid, p. 33
6. Hinsley *et al.*, p. 283
7. Ibid, p. 288
8. Public Record Office (PRO), WO 208/4294 (Scotland Papers)
9. Ibid
10. 'Instructions Regarding Disposal of Prisoners of War', HQ Southern Command, 19 September 1940. Held in the Wiltshire Record Office (WRO) Trowbridge, WRO F5/530/3: Wiltshire Constabulary Papers (Two vols 1939–47)
11. A.J. Barker, *Behind Barbed Wire* (Batsford, London, 1974), p. 66
12. R Garrett, *POW* (David & Charles, London, 1981), p. 167
13. Hinsley *et al*, pp. 282–3
14. Ibid, p. 205
15. PRO WO 208/4294
16. Ibid
17. Doug Richards, Letter to the Author, March 1996
18. Ibid
19. Ibid

Chapter Three

1. Siegfried Sassoon, 'In Barracks' from *Counter Attack*, 1918. Quoted in *Collins Dictionary of Military Quotations* (CDMQ), Trevor Royle (ed.) (HarperCollins, Glasgow, 1990), p. 135
2. L. Leete-Hodge, *The Story of Devizes* (Local Heritage Books, 1983)

3. Nigel Bray, *A Wiltshire Railway Remembered* (Picton Publishing, 1984)
4. *The Story of Devizes*, p. 40
5. Devizes Local Hist Prj
6. *The Story of Devizes*, p. 47
7. Devizes Local History Group, edited by Lorna Haycock, *How Devizes Won the War* (HDWW), 1994, p. 6
8. Journal of the Royal Wiltshire Regiment (RWR), July 1939, p. 51
9. *HDWW*, p. 7
10. RWR Journal, July 1939, p. 51
11. *HDWW*, p. 74
12. Wiltshire Home Guard Association, edited by Major E.A. Mackay, *History of the Wiltshire Home Guard*, 1946, p. 66
13. *HDWW*, pp. 73–4
14. John Perkins, Interview with the Author, January 1996
15. Nigel Bray, *A Wiltshire Railway Remembered*
16. Terry Gaylard, *Wiltshire Gazette*, 3 January 1980
17. Mrs A.M. Hehir, Interview with the Author, May 1995
18. *HDWW*, p. 78
19. Ian Samuel, *Doctor at Dunkirk with the 6th Field Ambulance at War* (Autolycus Publications, 1985), pp. 34–5
20. N.D.G. James, *Plain Soldiering. A history of the Armed Forces on Salisbury Plain* (The Hobnob Press, Salisbury, 1987), pp. 73–4
21. Harry Feinberg, Letter to the Author, February 1996
22. Quoted in *Rolling Together*, newsletter of the 4th US Armored Division, 1989, p. 32
23. Harry Feinberg, Letter to the Author, February 1996
24. Leonard 'Charlie' May, Interview with the Author, November 1995
25. Mrs Lil Painter, Interview with the Author, March 1996
26. *See* Southern Command Royal Engineers Works Services War Diary, March 1944 to January 1945, PRO WO 166/14219 and 15532
27. War Diary of 128 General Hospital, MDGH–128–0.1 (15 August to 30 September 1944) held in the National Archives, Washington DC, USA

Chapter Four

1. William E. Morris, CDMQ, p. 111
2. Home Office Letter, 9 September 1941, WRO F5/530/3
3. Home Office Letter, 10 May 1944, WRO F5/530/3
4. Home Office Letter, 23 August 1944, WRO F5/530/3
5. Ibid
6. Home Office Letter, 10 May 1944
7. *D-Day Then And Now*, vol. 2 (After the Battle, Battle of Britain Prints International Ltd, London, 1995), p. 487
8. B.L. Montgomery, *Normandy to the Baltic* (Hutchinson & Co., London, 1947), p. 53
9. Russell Miller, *Nothing Less Than Victory* (Michael Joseph, London, 1994), p. 389
10. Ibid, p. 392
11. Ronald H. Bailey, *Prisoners of War* (Time Life Books Inc., Chicago, 1981), p. 158
12. Winston Churchill, *The Second World War*, vol. IV (Cassell & Co. Ltd, London, 1951), p. 700
13. *Time Life*, p. 158
14. Gunter Schran, IWM Sound Archive Interview, 13582/3
15. Miriam Kochan, *Prisoners of England* (The Macmillan Press Ltd, London, 1980), p. 41
16. Ibid, p. 40

Chapter Five

1. John Buchan, CDMQ, p. 164
2. DPW 1A Files, PRO WO 165/61

3. Richard Hurn, Interviews with the Author, 1995 & 1996
4. Klaus Steffen, IWM Sound Archive Interview, 12577/4
5. Ron Priddle Archive
6. Joy Pride, Letter to the Author, November 1995
7. Mrs A.M. Hehir Interview
8. John Perkins, Interview with the Author, January 1996
9. David Knapman, Interview with the Author, January 1996
10. Home Office Letter, 23 August 1944, WRO F5/530/3
11. HQ Salisbury Plain and Dorset District, War Diary, November 1944, PRO WO 166/14443
12. Ibid, December 1944
13. Ibid
14. Ibid, January 1945
15. Emil Flemming, Interview with the Author, November 1995
16. Richard Garrett, *POW*, p. 163
17. Walter Herkstroeter, Interview with the Author, August 1995
18. Richard Garrett, *POW*, p. 164
19. John Perkins, Interview
20. Walter Herkstroeter, Interview
21. Emil Flemming, Interview

Chapter Six

1. Richard Lovelace (1618–58): 'To Althea from Prison'
2. Sir David Petrie to Sir Alexander Maxwell, October 1944, Constabulary Security File 1941–46, WRO F5/505/58
3. Richard Hurn, Interviews
4. The Shear Report, WRO F5/530/3
5. Ibid
6. CO 4 Wilts HG, Letter to Chief Constable, Devizes, WRO F5/530/3
7. POW Escape Report, WRO F5/530/3
8. Ibid
9. The Devizes Plot File, Scotland Papers, PRO WO 208/3651

10. Alfred Daltrey, Letter to the Author, October 1995
11. Mrs A. Toogood, Letter to the Author, March 1996
12. Scotland Papers, WO 208/3651
13. Ibid

Chapter Seven

1. *The London Cage*, p. 59
2. Robert Jackson, *A Taste of Freedom* (Arthur Barker Ltd, London, 1964), p. 20
3. Richard Hurn, Interviews
4. Scotland Papers, PRO WO 208/3651
5. See Samuel W. Mitcam, *Hitler's Legions* (Leo Cooper, London, 1985), pp. 458–9
6. Scotland Papers, PRO WO 208/3651
7. Richard Hurn, Interviews
8. Ibid
9. Quoted by Jean-Paul Pallud, *The Battle of the Bulge, Then and Now* (After the Battle, Battle of Britain Prints International Ltd, London, 1984), p. 63
10. Richard Hurn, Interviews
11. Scotland Papers, PRO WO 208/3651
12. Ibid
13. SPDD War Diaries, WO 166/14443
14. Ibid
15. Ibid
16. 6th Airborne Armoured Recce Regiment War Diary, December 1944, PRO WO 171/435
17. Dr Tony Leake, Letter to the Author, November 1995
18. Jim Wheeler, Telephone conversation with the Author, November 1995
19. Frank Ockenden, Letters to the Author, December 1995 & January 1996
20. T.M. Hopkins, Letter and telephone conversation with the Author, January 1996

21. Frank Ockenden, Letters
22. Peter Roberts, Letters to the Author, November 1995
23. Harry Gosling, Letter to the Author, January 1996
24. Colonel Alistair Wilson, Letter to the Author, November 1995

Chapter Eight

1. General Thomas Jackson in *Stonewall Jackson and the American Civil War*, Henderson, vol. 1 (1898) CDMQ, p. 33
2. Walter Chebatoris, Letters to the Author, June & December 1995
3. Sidney Curry via Arthur McKechnie, Letters to the Author, February & March 1996
4. Richard Hurn, Interviews
5. Mrs Mary Grafton, Interview with the Author, September 1995
6. Scotland Papers, PRO WO 208/3651
7. Ibid
8. Ibid
9. Storch Interrogation, Scotland Papers, PRO WO 208/3651
10. Wunderlich Interrogation, Scotland Papers, PRO WO 208/3651
11. Ibid
12. Ibid
13. Scotland Papers, PRO WO 208/3651
14. See Keessings Contemporary Archives, 22 December 1944
15. *Daily Express*, 18 December 1944
16. Via Walter Chebatoris, Paper unidentified
17. Polish Guard Companies Summary, Polish Government In Exile, London, via the Polish Sikorski Institute & Library, Blackfriars, London
18. Ibid
19. Pawel Bechler, Interview with the Author, November 1995
20. Ibid

21. SPDD War Diary, February 1945, PRO WO 166/16514
22. Richard Hurn, Interviews
23. Pawel Bechler, Interview
24. Richard Hurn, Interviews
25. 'Charlie' May, Interview

Chapter Nine

1. Captain Sir Basil Liddell Hart, CDMQ, p. 190
2. WRO F5/530/3
3. S.E. Brook, Letter to the Author, October 1995
4. Nora Hamilton, *The Black & The Grey*, BBC Pebble Mill, 1984, via the Peter Everett Archive
5. Ibid, Jenny MacGregor
6. Lawrence McCulloch, Letters to the Author, November 1995
7. Henry Faulk, *Group Captives* (Chatto & Windus, London, 1977), p. 66
8. Werner Busse, Letter to the Author, January 1996
9. Gunter Schran, IWM Interview, 13582/3
10. *Revue International de la Croix–Rouge*, vol. LXXV, No. 503, Geneva, July 1944, p. 517
11. MI–19A CSDIC Report, 19 December 1944, PRO WO 208/3530
12. Ibid
13. Ibid
14. Ibid
15. Albert Mai, BBC Interview, 1983, via the Peter Everett Archive
16. Peter Everett Archive
17. 7 PGC Weekly Report, 13 January 1945, Polish Sikorski Institute & Library, London
18. Richard Hurn, Interviews
19. Jim Gaiger, BBC Interview, 1983, via the Peter Everett Archive
20. *Group Captives*, p. 110
21. Summary of Evidence, The Rosterg Murder File, PRO WO 208/4633

22. *The London Cage*, p. 62
23. Albert Mai, BBC Interview

Chapter Ten

1. J. Glenn Grey, CDMQ, p. 148
2. For a full account *see* George Hume, *Spectrum*, 18 December 1994
3. Summary of Evidence, PRO WO 208/4633
4. Ibid, Bultmann statement
5. Ibid
6. Ibid, Von Goll statement
7. Ibid, Froetsch statement
8. Ibid, Heubner statement
9. Ibid, Vollstedt statement
10. Ibid, Bultmann statement
11. Ibid
12. Ibid, Schmidt statement
13. Ibid, Huebner statement
14. Ibid, Lergenmuller statement
15. Albert Mai, BBC Interview

Chapter Eleven

1. Geoffrey Household; 'Rogue Male' (1939)
2. Scottish Command Operational Instruction, PRO WO 166/16382
3. WRO F5/530/3
4. Hansard, 20 February 1945, col. 609
5. Ibid, col 610
6. *Thresholds of Peace*, p. 123
7. Herbert Sulzbach, *Total War to Total Trust* (Oswald Wolff, London, 1976), p. 10
8. Herbert Sulzbach, IWM Sound Archive Interview, 4338/3
9. Sulzbach to Liddell Hart, 11 May 1945, Liddell Hart Centre for Military Archives, LH 1/666
10. Colonel A. Wilson, Comrie Notes, the Peter Everett Archive
11. Ibid
12. Ibid
13. Ibid
14. The Rt Hon Lord Wheatley PC,

One Man's Judgement (Butterworths, London, 1987), pp. 91–2
15. Alexander Budge, *In Enemy Hands* (Privately published, Wick, 1990), p. 12
16. Ibid
17. For a full account *see The John O'Groats Journal*, April 1994
18. Hansard, 24 April 1945, col. 659

Chapter Twelve

1. CDMQ, p. 70
2. Judge Advocate General's Papers, PRO WO 213/65
3. The *Swindon Evening Advertiser* (*SEA*), 3 July 1945, front page
4. Ibid
5. Ibid, back page
6. Summary of Evidence, PRO WO 208/4633, Huebner statement
7. Ibid, Lergenmuller statement
8. Ibid, Bultmann statement
9. Ibid
10. *SEA*, 3 July 1945, back page
11. Summary of Evidence, Schmidt statement
12. Ibid
13. Ibid
14. Ibid
15. Ibid, Merfeld testimony
16. *SEA*, 4 July 1945, front page
17. *SEA*, 5 July 1945, back page
18. *SEA*, 6 July 1945, back page
19. Ibid
20. Ibid
21. *SEA*, 7 July 1945, back page
22. Ibid
23. Ibid
24. *SEA*, 9 July 1945, back page
25. Ibid
26. *SEA*, 11 July 1945, back page
27. Ibid
28. *SEA*, 12 July 1945, back page
29. Pallme Koenig, note to Scotland, PRO WO 208/4633

Chapter Thirteen

1. J. MacMullen, CDMQ, p. 184
2. Letter DPW to JAG, 18 July 1945, PRO WO 83/87
3. Letter JAG to HQ London District, 23 July 1945, PRO WO 83/87
4. Albert Pierrepoint, BBC Interview, 1983
5. Ibid
6. Bienek note, PRO WO 208/4633
7. The Peter Everett Archive
8. Ibid
9. Sulzbach to Liddell Hart, 11 May 1945, LH 1/666
10. *Total War to Total Trust*, p. 12
11. Ibid, pp. 14–15
12. Ibid, p. 21
13. PID, Foreign Office Files, PRO FO 393/106
14. King to Wilson, 19 July 1945, PRO FO 393/106
15. King report on Comrie Camp, 24 December 1945, PRO FO 393/106
16. Devizes 410 German PW Work Camp Report, 12 April 1946, PRO FO 939/318
17. Devizes Report, 4 May 1946, PRO FO 939/318
18. Arthur McKechnie, Letters to the Author, February & March 1996
19. Devizes Report, 6 August 1946, PRO FO 939/318
20 Undated letter, PRO FO 939/318

Public Record Office
Research Notes

The Public Record Office is a national treasure. No true researcher can prepare a book or paper without first consulting Kew. During the research for this book, it was necessary for me to consult a myriad files and documents to piece together the true story. These are the references I consulted:

From the Cabinet Office Papers:
CAB 81/126 & 127: Chiefs of Staff Committee
CAB 93: War Cabinet Home Defence Committee
CAB 100/12 & 13: War Cabinet Daily Situation Reports
CAB 121/230: Joint Intelligence Staff Papers
CAB 121/236: CSDIC Papers (1940–44)
CAB 121/300: CSDIC Papers Special Intelligence – POWs

From the Prime Minister's Office Papers:
PREM 3, 4, 7 & 10

From the Air Ministry Papers:
AIR 25/565 & 567: 27 Training Group – Cirencester
AIR 28/966: RAF Yatesbury Station Records Books
AIR 29/719 & 729: No. 2 & No. 9 Radio Schools – Yatesbury

From the War Office Files:
WO 32(91A)/11121: Re-education of POWs (1944)
WO 32(91A)/11699: Concerning Anti-Nazi POWs
WO 32(91A)/14552: POW Deaths (Released for the author)
WO 71, 81 to 93: JAG Papers
WO 165/37: MI-5 (Permits)
WO 165/38: MI-8 (September 1939 – February 1942)
WO 165/39: MI-9 (1944)
WO 165/40: MI-11 (1941–43)
WO 165/41: MI-19 (1941–45)
WO 165/42: MI-12 (1940–45)
WO 165/43: MI Liaison (1941–43)
WO 165/67 to 71: POW Directorate Papers
WO 166/14174: GHQ Home Command 1944 (G Files)
WO 166/14175: GHQ Home Command 1994 (Int. Files)
WO 166/14217: Southern Command 1944 (G Files)
WO 166/14218: Southern Command 1944 (Ops Files)
WO 166/14219: Southern Command 1944 (A Files)

WO 166/14226: Scottish Command 1944 (G Files)
WO 166/14227: Scottish Command 1944 (Ops Files)
WO 166/14228: Scottish Command 1944 (Int. Files)
WO 166/14443: HQ Salisbury Plain and Dorset District 1944
WO 166/14445: East Scotland District 1944 (G Files)
WO 166/14446: East Scotland District 1944 (AQ Files)
WO 166/14447: East Scotland District 1944 (Engr. Files)
WO 166/14571: HQ Corsham Garrison 1944
WO 166/15091: War Diary – 30th Devons (1944)
WO 166/15179: War Diary – 7th R Wilts (1944)
WO 166/15964: War Diary – 24 Group, Pioneer Corps
WO 166/15970: War Diary – 30 Group, Pioneer Corps
WO 166/15980: War Diary – 80 Group, Pioneer Corps
WO 166/16091: War Diary – 389 Pioneer Company
WO 166/16271: War Diary – 175 CMP Company
WO 166/16690: War Diary – 46 AA Brigade
WO 166/16835: War Diary – 5 Calibration Troop RA
WO 166/16382: Scottish Command 1945 (G Files)
WO 166/16383: Scottish Command 1945 (A Files)
WO 166/16384: Scottish Command 1945 (Q Files)
WO 166/16385: Scottish Command 1945 (Int. Files)
WO 166/16491 to 94: London District 1945
WO 166/16514: Salisbury Plain and Dorset District 1945
WO 166/16516: East Scotland District 1945 (G Files)
WO 166/16517: East Scotland District 1945 (AQ Files)
WO 166/16518: East Scotland District 1945 (Engr. Files)
WO 171/425: HQ 6th Airborne Division (G Files)
WO 171/435: War Diary – 6th Ab. Recce Regt
WO 171/1240: War Diary – 8 Para Battalion
WO 179/2608: First Canadian Army Intelligence
WO 199/404 to 409: POW Employment Files
WO 199/422 to 424: POW Escort Files
WO 199/3303: Special POW Interrogations (Closed)
WO 199/3304: Southern Command Cypher Messages (Closed)
WO 208/3530: Comrie Camp Reports
WO 208/3652 to 3660: London Cage Files
WO 208/4139 to 4177: CSDIC Reports and Papers
WO 208/4295: Scotland Papers
WO 208/4633: Rosterg Murder File
WO 213/59 to 65: Further JAG Papers
WO 307: POW Information Bureau Files

Index